Rethinking Religion
Studies in the Hellenistic Process

OPUSCULA GRAECOLATINA
(Supplementa Musei Tusculani)
Edenda curavit Ivan Boserup
vol. 30

Rethinking Religion:
Studies in the Hellenistic Process

edited by

Jørgen Podemann Sørensen

MUSEUM TUSCULANUM PRESS
COPENHAGEN 1989

BL
730
.R470
1989

© The authors and Museum Tusculanum Press
Printed in Denmark by Special-Trykkeriet Viborg a-s
ISBN 87-7289-079-7
ISSN 0107-8089

PREFACE

The origin of the present dossier of studies is a symposium, held in April 1984 by the Institute for the History of Religions at the University of Copenhagen, on the occasion of professor Ugo Bianchi's visit. The intention to publish the symposium ripened during the rest of 1984, and to the original presentations were added the contribution by *Per Bilde* on Roman Mithraism and the editor's *Attis or Osiris?*. The manuscripts were ready in 1985, but for reasons mainly economical their publication was delayed till now. The benevolent reader of 1988 or later is kindly asked to bear these early origins in mind.

Jørgen Podemann Sørensen

CONTENTS

Jørgen Podemann Sørensen: *Introduction* 5
Ugo Bianchi: *Mystery Cult and Gnostic Religiosity in Antiquity* ... 11
Jørgen Podemann Sørensen: *The Myth of Attis: Structure and Mysteriosophy* 23
Per Bilde: *The Meaning of Roman Mithraism* 31
Søren Giversen: *Hermetic Communities?* 49
Jørgen Verner Hansen: *Adamas and the Four Illuminators in Sethian Gnosticism* 55
Jørgen Podemann Sørensen: *Attis or Osiris?* 73
Karin Weinholt: *The Gateways of Judaism. From Simon the Just to Rabbi Akiba* 87

INTRODUCTION

by Jørgen Podemann Sørensen

The first students of Hellenism and of what we shall call the Hellenistic process were the Christian fathers of the 2nd – 4th centuries. As it is well known, although they were part of this very process, they insisted on viewing it from outside, from the standpoint of a religion destined to reveal all heathenism as a human folly — or even better: as devilish measures to seduce mankind and distort the order of the divine plan for the salvation of the world. In so doing they treated other religions largely on the premises of their own: The philosophical aspects of Hellenism they would measure in terms of Christian theology and bring out as *falsa opinio*; the myths told by their fellow hellenists they would treat in terms of newly fashioned ideas of time: as history and bring them out as absurd stories tracing the origin of the present condition in a monstrous and inconceivable series of events. The ritual aspects of contemporary non-Christian religions they often saw as superfluous dealings with nature, with the elements etc. And anyway they represented ritual as based on belief, i.e. on *falsa opinio* and therefore either ridiculous or blasphemous.

They did, however, view Hellenism as a process, as a temporal sequence of events and shifting constellations, ultimately governed by the divine plan for the salvation of the world, but with Christianity and a host of heathen cults and creeds as *dramatis personae*. The dialectic of the process they saw and made visible was one of apparent similarity versus real, radical exclusiveness. At times they even went as far as exaggerating the similarity of Christianity and heathen cults in order to present in still sharper terms the radical exclusiveness and uniqueness of their religion.

Even if something of this dramatic dialectics has survived in reprinted theological textbooks, this is not the approach of modern scholarship. The meticulous collection of source material both archaeological and textual, inaugurated above all by Franz Cumont, has established a far more varied and detailed picture of Hellenism — and in addition, progress in the studies of the oriental religions, especially Judaism and ancient Egyptian religion, has somewhat alleviated a problem still envisaged by Cumont in 1929:[1]

> Nous sommes encore loin de pouvoir souder solidement tous les anneaux de cette longue chaîne; les orientalistes et les philologues classiques ne peuvent encore se tendre la main par-dessus la Méditerranée.

Still today not a few links of this long chain are missing, and some of the oriental cults we shall probably never know in their prehellenistic shape. But in other cases the material basis for more specific and detailed studies of the continuity as well as the discontinuity of prehellenistic and Hellenistic religion is there. In others words, the Hellenistic process, the historical process in which oriental and Greco-roman traditions are subject to change according to environmental conditions such as cultural milieu and social, economic, and political constellations, may now be approached at least in case-studies.

It was also Cumont who spoke about this process as 'une lente métamorphose'[2] — above all in the development of the political institutions of imperial Rome, but intimately connected with a general process of orientalization in all aspects of culture. The transformation of religious beliefs and practice could thus be seen not as an isolated phenomenon, but as part of this general development, favouring, and favoured by, the transformation of society and culture. This essentially modern view of a cultural process is among the greatest merits of its author, but in his idea of an orientalization of the European mind Cumont is definitely a child of his time:

> Les chimères de l'astrologie et de la magie se font accepter des meilleurs esprits. La philosophie prétends de plus en plus s'inspirer de la sagesse fabuleuse de la Chaldée ou de l'Egypte. La raison, lasse de chercher la vérité, abdique et croit la trouver dans une révélation primitive, conservée dans les mystères des barbares. La logique de la Grèce s'ingénie à coordonner en un ensemble les traditions confuses des sacerdoces asiatiques.[3]

Like *Tychiades* in Lucian's *Philopseudes* he is astonished to find credulity and monstrous fables even among prominent heirs of the classical Greco-roman tradition. Well versed in the classical tradition and with direct access to the European mind he had to ascribe such irrational mysteries and monstrosities to oriental influence.

At least on the level of style this basic antagonism of classical reason and the fabulous Orient conveys to the work of Cumont something of the dramatic quality also found in patristic literature. Throughout his repeated excersises on the rhetoric of antagonism it should be borne in mind, however, that behind the violent clashes of *mos maiorum* and the new oriental religions there was a gradual and much less spectacular *rethinking* of religious traditions, both in the Orient and in Europe, to which Cumont's own term, 'une lente métamorphose', would apply perfectly well. This process of rethinking and re-formulating traditional religion is certainly not limited to the Hellenistic period. Such a process goes on within any culture, meeting the demands of changing conditions, and often inspired by culture contacts. In the Hellenistic period, both culture contacts and change in economic and social conditions reach an intensity unprecedented in the ancient world. No doubt the rapid changes and the amount of religious innovations were experienced by many very much in the way described by Lucian's *Tychiades* and still, to some extent, by Cumont: as an Asiatic flue, a sudden madness, or, on the part of some orientals, as the boasting *Besserwissen* of the ruling Greeks.[4] — The historian, however, must account also for the continuity which, after all, makes change possible: the analogies and homologies of the old and the new, the reinterpretations of tradition, and the delicate shifts of meaning when a tradition looses its context or is employed in a new social and cultural setting.

It is to such traces of the rethinking of traditional religion, within the framework of the Hellenistic process at large, that the present dossier of studies is devoted. Professor *Bianchi*'s presentation shows exactly such a process in Greek religious thought, leading from 'mystic trends' as early as the sixth century B.C. *via* mystery cults to Hellenistic mysteriosophy and gnostic religiosity. It does so by means of comparative historical thematizations which enable us to recognize the continuity of the process, but at the same time exhibit the distinction — or the break of tradition — between e.g. mystery religion and mysteriosophy. Within the abstract framework of these generalized notions it becomes possible to account for the gradual introduction of more than one important Hellenistic trend, e.g. dualism.

The anthropological, but also cosmological and ontological, dualism of mysteriosophy is also an important issue in the next contribution, by the editor, on the structure of the Attis myth. The mysteriosophic reinterpretation of the Attis-Cybele motif could, with only very delicate changes, transform a myth designed to account for the ritual competence of priests of Cybele into a soteriological paradigm of definitely dualist stock. Dualism could be introduced by analogy with the structure of a premysteriosophic myth.

The mysteriosophic revolution, however, should not be thought of as a *coup d'état* imposing, from a certain date, a radical dualism on all members of society. Dualism was a consequence drawn by philosophers and men of letters. It was rooted, no doubt, in a much more common experience, but in dealing with the mystery religions the continuum shown by prof. Bianchi should always be kept in mind. An important additional point is made by *Per Bilde* in this volume. Basing his general interpretation of Mithraism and its soteriology on central and omnipresent features, the Mithraeum and the bull-slaying scene, he reaches the conclusion that Roman Mithraism was a this-worldly and monistic religion. In this perspective the literary sources, notably *Origen* and *Porphyry*, appear as the results of dualistic, philosophical reinterpretations: the rethinking of Mithraism in Platonic and Neopythagorean categories.

Of crucial importance in Bilde's distinction between the central and the mysteriosophic trends in Mithraism is the well-established knowledge we have about the social status of its adepts. Such a knowledge is, however, not available for all Hellenistic religions. The gnostic trends, and Hermetism in particular, seem almost without any social context. Who were the Hermetists? — and did Hermetic communities ever exist? This is the question taken up by *Søren Giversen* in an examination of the Hermetic tractates. Since it was written, its important and fundamental questions have been treated on a much broader basis by *Garth Fowden* in his excellent *The Egyptian Hermes*,[5] but Giversen's paper remains valuable for its balanced account of what can be deduced from the tractates themselves.

In gnosticism, as it is represented in the Coptic gnostic writings, rethinking was a *modus vivendi*. Not only are some of them new intertations (*exegesis*) of Old Testament texts, purporting to give the true sense or even the true story behind the traditional texts,[6] but also the theological and mythological systems so prominent in this literature were constantly rethought and reshaped. The chains of emanation, with their personnel of Aeons and *anthropoi*, *Sophia*s and Saviours, occur in multiple variants and combinations, each one rethinking and reformulating the immense distance between the ineffable God and the present human condition, but at the same time forming a soteriological paradigm. To perceive the unity and account for the diversities of these variant systems is much more than a question of diligent indexing of gnostic items; it involves an inquiry into the nature of gnostic rethinking like the one undertaken by *Jørgen Verner Hansen* on the subject of the four *phosteres* in Sethian gnosticism.

The rethinking of religion was, however, not only a matter of innovation or adaptation to a new cultural and social framework; it was also a matter of preserving religious traditions and patterns of life in front of political and cultural pressure. The history of Judaism in the Hellenistic period is an excellent example: there were the violent clashes of culture and religion, oppression and resistance, but also, in the rabbinic literature examined by *Karin Weinholt*, a much less spectacular rethinking of Jewish religious tradition, which kept it alive by redefining it on Jewish premises.

In these various ways the title theme and its role in the Hellenistic process is exemplified and explored in the case-studies here assembled. It has been the task of this introduction to point to their common denominator, the rethinking of religion, as an important issue in Hellenistic studies, too important to disappear in vague, general descriptions like 'orientalization' or 'hellenization'. Each of these studies has, however, virtues of its own, to the discovery of which the reader is now invited.

NOTES:

1. Franz Cumont: *Les réligions orientales dans le paganisme romain*, Paris 1929, p. 28.
2. *ibid.*, p. 4.
3. *ibid.*, p. 9.
4. Cf. e.g. the XVIth tractate of the *Corpus Hermeticum*, 1-2, for an explicit statement to this effect.
5. Garth Fowden: *The Egyptian Hermes*. Cambridge 1986.
6. An excellent example is *The Hypostasis of the Archons*; see the instructive analysis by Ingvild Gilhus: *The Nature of the Archons*, Wiesbaden 1985 (Studies in Oriental Religions; 12), p. 21-36.

MYSTERY CULT AND GNOSTIC RELIGIOSITY IN ANTIQUITY

by Ugo Bianchi

Man, God and Destiny: this is a central issue of religious, and generally human concern, and also a topic which has given rise to much discussion among historians of religion. Perhaps not all of us will be prepared to share Prof. Widengren's views about the essence of the 'High God' of several religions, both 'primitive' and literate, as being God-Destiny, an identification which led him to classify in the same phenomenological category, that of 'monism', figures as radically different in character as the great God of Mazdeanism, Ahura Mazda, and the semi-personal hypostasis of Time-Destiny in the Iranian religio-philosophical speculation, namely Zurvan *akarana*, 'Boundless Time'. But we must recognize that the intimate connection between Deity, the High God, and destiny — human and cosmic — is a central issue of religious phenomenology. The African religions, as it was pointed out by Widengren in his book *Hochgottglaube im alten Iran* (1938), are good examples for this. Moreover, there are expressions in various languages and religious contexts, which are classical formulations of these connections between God and destiny, formulations that are similar in character: the Greek Διὸς αἶσα, 'the destiny of Zeus', in the sense of the destiny which is established by Zeus, or at least the destiny which is intimately connected with Zeus and his administration of the world; the Roman *fata deorum* or *fata Iovis*; the Iranian *Zamān-i Ohrmazd*, i.e. the Time, the Destiny as appointed by Ohrmazd, the High God of Zoroastrianism,[1] down to the Chinese *Tien Ming*, the decree or the order of God Heaven.

It is our intention in this presentation to gain an insight into a particular aspect of the general issue 'man and his destiny' in Greek religion, and particularly in Greek mystic religion, — which will lead us also to a more articulate definition and categorization of that branch of Greek spiritual experience, as well as of the ontology and anthropology of gnosticism.

No doubt, it is commonplace among classicists that Greek religion, the religion of Homer and Hesiod, the religion of Walter Otto's *Die Götter Griechenlands*, in other terms: what we call the 'Olympian' religion, was not very interested in the afterlife — in contradistinction to those mystic trends of religiosity which were also active in Greece. Of course, such a schematic distinction between *Olympian* religion and *mystic* religion in Greece, has much in its favor.[2] Formulating that rather rough opposition as a working hypothesis, we cannot deny that the basic Greek concept of destiny, *moira*, is commonplace in Greek religious ideology at large, either Olympian or mystic, and that the respective ideal associations of that term are commonplace as well. Thus we could use the history of the term *moira* as an Ariadne's thread in order to unravel the complexities of Greek basic attitudes toward death, destiny and afterlife. So for example, whilst in Homer and Hesiod *moira* is the expression of a destiny or a fate which is appointed in a series of fundamentally unconnected 'portions' or 'shares' allotted to prominent or less prominent individuals,[3] and this in the context of a conception of destiny static and, so to say, 'cold', it happens that on the other side, in the Orphic tablets of Southern Italy[4] *moira* is dynamically opposed to the blessings of an afterlife which is viewed mystically, in the framework of a clearly outlined and 'warmly' experienced soteriology.

Thus the case of *moira* indicates clearly that perhaps already around 500 B.C. the same term and, *mutatis mutandis*, the same concept could function in different, or even contrasting spiritual and ideological contexts. For one, this could confirm that too simplistic an interpretation of the complexities of Greek religion and culture, and of the opposition between 'Olympian' and 'mystic', could be misleading. So for example, a historical-cultural explanation which would choose to schematically contrast an Olympian religion of aristocratic invaders and a chthonian-mystic religion of the conquered, would be outdated. Things are at the same time more simple and more complicated. Similarly, a too simple opposition between Indoeuropeans and 'Mediterranean' races in the same connection would remain far from meeting the actual complexities of the cultural and racial stratifications and clashes in proto-historical Greece. After all, and without drawing into a-historical functionalism, the functional aspect of the coexistence in archaic Greece of both attitudes concerning *moira* is not to be neglected.

As it seems to me, it appears clearly from these few indications that a study of the concepts and the experiences of destiny and of salvation in Greece cannot be carried out apart from an articulated religio-historical and comparative-historical thematization. A merely bi-dimensional and a-historical phenomenology would be out of place here. This methodological warning applies both for the analysis of the opposition 'Olympian religion' versus 'mystic religion' in Greece, and for the internal articulation of Greek mystic religion itself.

At the Strasbourg conference of the International Association for the History of Religions in 1964,[5] I had the opportunity to submit a concise typology of Greek mystic religion, starting from a general definition of the very term 'mystic' (in the sense of *to mystikon, ta mystika*), as it applies to pre-Christian Greece. As a result of a series of conceptual refinements based on empirical observation, my own definition of the religious quantity we may call *to mystikon* reads as follows: In the religio-historical context of pre-Christian Greece and the surrounding Mediterranean area in pre-Christian times, mystic are all conceptions and practices which imply a vividly experienced interference and participation of realms and of destinies between what is divine and what is human. This interference and this participation take place in the context of a 'warm' mythical-ritual structure according to which a god (a 'mystic' god) or an otherwise divine or celestial element undergoes a fate (that is, a typical vicissitude, often cyclically repetitive) of fall and reintegration or of absence and 'return', a return, as we shall see, very different from a 'resurrection'. Moreover, this divine vicissitude or fate of the god is not without consequences for the destiny of those men and women ritually or ideologically interested in it.

On the contrary, 'Olympian' are the conceptions and the ritual patterns in which, as in a cold structure, there is no real and intimate participation between the human and the divine realms and destinies, in the sense that the gods can leave for some time their abodes and privileges. Some Olympians in the Iliad do so — but without really sharing in the destinies of their respective human sons or protégés, whom they abandon just one instant before death reaches them. Equally, merely Olympian is the conception that some particular heroes can be transferred, without having experienced death, to the

Islands of the Blessed or to Heaven, — as if they were metamorphosized into a paradisiac condition of life, which is now their privilege. But these are just exceptions which confirm the rule, that of a mankind which, in the Olympian conception, is given a general destiny of death, outside any specific soteriological perspective.

Clearly, the Olympian worldview knows also the idea of a destiny of the gods, as it is to be seen from the Hesiodean Theogony.[6] We find here numerous *Götterdämmerungen*: Ouranos, Kronos, the Titans, the Giants, Typhon. All these primordial or chaotic figures are struck by a destiny not very different from the *moira* of a human hero in the specific context of epic poetry. But this does not mean, of course, that in the Olympian religion, not even in the Hesiod's *Götterdämmerungen*, gods and men are really comparable, as far as their destinies are concerned. On the contrary, as we have seen, the fundamental concept of the Olympian religion implies a sharp and irreconciliable, typological opposition between gods and men. But what is important for the present purpose is that both series of destinies, those of the epic, Olympian heroes and of the epic, Olympian gods (those which experience a fate) belong to what we called a 'cold' structure, far removed from that concept of vicissitudes, of fall and rescue, of death and life, absence and return, which is typical for the 'warm' structure of Greek mystic religion, that warm structure in which, as we have said, the divine and the human spheres interfere, and the vicissitudes of the god (or of the divine soul) are the conceptual and factual motivation for this interference. Think, for the moment, of that typically 'mystic' deity, Dionysos, and the specific kind of divine-human interference he provokes, called *enthousiasmos*.

We come now to the proper subject-matter of this lecture, a categorization within the general concept of 'mystic' religion in Greece. First of all, we have to distinguish between the broader concept of 'mystic', according to the already given definition of it, and more qualified forms of Dionysism which are not initiatory (so e.g. the rituals of Dionysiac frenzy, such cults as those of Lerna and Delphi, or the Beotian *Agrionia*).[7] Then we come to the mystery religion, as exemplified by the Eleusinian mysteries, which can be thus defined: a mythical-ritual structure in which, on the basis of an ancient pattern of seasonal fertility implying the ritualization of the loss and the 'invention' of a chthonic god, a group of initiands is given lasting privileges in a context of strict esotericism. These privileges mean a good life in this world and a special blessing and a friendship with the Nether Gods in a chthonic afterlife, according to the 'sweet hopes' which, intimated in a kind of liturgical proclamation (*olbioi*...),[8] accompany the initiate during his life. As for the rite itself, it takes place in a specially appointed sanctuary, inaccessible to those not engaged in the rites, at fixed times (this, at least, for Eleusis). As for the relationship with the political institutions, we can omit it here, since the situation in (historical) Eleusis was completely specific. The participation in the ritual — it would seem — was preeminently visual, but it implied also (at Eleusis and in the Metroac mysteries) a material contact with the sacred objects on the part of the initiand, and a participation in the god's vicissitudes symbolized in a sacred representation. So far we can guess, this participation did not imply a divinization or a divine nature of the initiate, but only an overcoming of the negative aspect of death, on the basis of the familiarity with the mystery deities granted by initiation. According to this, the initiate's life is not fated to submit to the common destiny when crossing the threatening threshold of death. To be sure, that initiate undergoes the common experience of death; but this, with all its pains and all its agony, is for him an experience of liberation and of access to light in a subterranean Elysium.[9]

We are perfectly conscious that this description of 'mystery religion' is largely dependent on the documentation concerning Eleusis and those late-antique mystery cults (Metroac and Isiac) which were heavily inspired by some aspects of the Eleusinian celebration. But this typology of a mystery cult is far from being a matter of course. It cannot be tested against another famous 'mystery cult', that of Samothrake, where no ultra-mundane blessing for the initiate and no particular connection with seasonal rituals are mentioned in the relevant documentation. True, we can guess for them the existence of a mythological pattern connected with a particular fate of some deity or hero, and that 'salvation' — be it only in this life and concerning the dangers of sea — was a central element in those *mysteria*. All in all, it will be wise to suspend the judgement concerning the Greek mysteria *in toto*, and to limit our typology to Eleusis and to those mystery cults which were in all probability inspired by some typical aspects of the Eleusinian ritual of initiation. In this case, we cannot abstain from emphasizing the coalescence, in those mystery cults, of some aspects of the old fertility cults, implying the periodical reenactment of the destiny of some (chthonic) deity undergoing a mythical vicissitude, and of the typical rite of initiation giving access to a state of blessing, being a remedy against the fate of death and the *ponoi* and *pathēmata* of this life.

So much for the mystery religion, particularly that of the Eleusinian mysteries.

We come now to our third category, that of mysteriosophy, which we distinguish from the category of mystery religion. On one hand, mysteriosophy — in other words: Orphism — is a continuation of the liberating effect of mystery religion. On the other hand it deepens and transcends it, far beyond its limits, so that we can speak of a true 'mysteriosophical revolution'. A famous passage from *de anima* of Plutarch is significant here. He is describing the access of the soul, after much pain and agony, to the Elysian fields in an afterworld; but he describes it in mysteriosophic colors.[10] In this perspective, those who are living this earthly life, particularly those 'non-initiated', who do not have faith in the other world, are really dead; only those coming to the other world with this faith are really alive. We can say that this text is, so to say, intermediate between mystery religion and mysteriosophy. The soul does not seem 'divine' in its nature, but earthly life is really death, in comparison with the other.

Thus, according to our definition, the notion of vicissitude of the god or of the soul is crucial, both in mystery religion and in mysteriosophy. The difference is that in the mysteriosophical-Orphic experience, the subject and object of that vicissitude of fall and rescue are not exclusively the mystery god, but also — and primarily — the divine or heavenly soul, that is a soul which is consubstantial with the divine, a soul fallen into a corporeal world and a corporeal body wherefrom she has to rescue herself in order to be reintegrated in the divine realm or in the divine essence to which she originally belonged. That essence which is *ousia*, both in the Platonic and the gnostic sense of the world.

A corollary of this is that in this particular type of mystic experience and belief we call mysteriosophy, the notion of a positive and soterical character of the seasonal ritual of the fertility rites (and also of the autumnal mysteries of Eleusis) is changed into the negative concept of the 'cycle', a cycle which is not culminating in life, in the promotion of life, but which means on the contrary the culmination of death. There is a painful, repetitive cycle of births and rebirths, in the realm of a *genesis* which means also *phthora*. Of course, the fertility cults and the mystery cults know already the notion of some painful destiny of the god, of the dying and dead (i.e. not really resurrecting) god of the type of an Attis or an Adonis.[11] But the difference remains. In the 'mystic' rites of fertility, implying a vicissitude of a mystic god, the cycle, periodically culminating in the ritual departure (rather than in the return) of the god, is something sad and painful, accompanied by lamentation. But it remains true that the cycle itself is beneficent to the territory and the community living in it; and the same applies for the mysteries. The opposite holds true for mysteriosophy. We find here the paradoxical formulation, quoted or expressed by Euripides: 'who can know whether life is death and death is life?',[12] a typical and, as already said, revolutionary formulation. This is the message of the Orphics, and of Plato, a message already in existence in the sixth century B.C., a period which was called 'the axial age'.

Of very central importance for the mysteriosophic experience is the notion I propose to call the 'previous sin', in contradistinction to the Christian notion of 'original sin'.[13] We can define the 'previous sin' as follows: it is a guilt, or a bare accident, or both of them, which is conceived to have taken place primordially, in a kind of prologue in heaven, at the level of the divine or at the level of the cosmogonical principles, -- a guilt or an accident which is considered as having caused man and his bodily constitution to be brought into existence; a guilt, say, which is not only pre-human but also pre-cosmic. It is clear that this origin of sin or a fateful accident at the very level of the divine or of the first principles, before man's bodily existence, implies something which, in the most radical cases, is very similar to that 'split in the divine' where Quispel[14] sees one of the more specific marks of gnostic experience. We shall return to this. What is important now is to remark that the notion of the 'previous guilt' is a dualistic notion, that is, it implies the 'doctrine of the two principles which, coeternal or not, found the existence of what exists or appears to exist in this world'.[15] More specifically, the dualism of mysteriosophy is above all an anthropological dualism. But it is theological and ontological too, as it is demonstrated in Empedocles, where the primordial fall of the soul is only an *epiphenomenon* of the radical and dialectical opposition between the two metaphysical opposites, Love and Discord. In other cases, less radical, the previous sin is to be considered as a second principle, causing man to be brought into corporeal existence.

Before coming to gnosticism and to more detailed examples of 'previous guilt' we would like to emphasize that there is no mutual compatibility between 'previous sin' (and anthropological dualism) on the one hand, and 'Olympian religion' on the other. Think only of the Prometheus' myth, where, at variance with what happens with the mysteriosophic idea of 'previous sin', there is no continuity between the sinner and the victim, in the sense that Prometheus is not a man nor a prototype of man. Prometheus is an entity apart from mankind, he is the Titanic Trickster.[16] Thus, it would seem that some kind of continuity between the pre-cosmic, pre-human and pre-corporeal sinner and the punished, corporeal man is specific for mysteriosophy.[17] This does not exclude that the figure of Prometheus could also be used in mysteriosophical contexts, e.g. in those late-antique narratives and artistic figurations on sarcophagi where the Titan acts as the demiurge of the body of man or of woman, in the style of a gnostic Demiurge, whilst the soul creeps into the newly formed body coming from Heaven, through the hands of Athena, the representative of the wisdom and power of Zeus.

The connection of the mysteriosophic experience we have described, with the gnostic experience is too clear to be insisted upon in this context. Think only of the *sōma-sēma* conception, both mysteriosophic-Orphic and gnostic. We would prefer to insist on some characteristic features of the notion and the experience of 'previous sin', a concept — as we said — to be clearly distinguished from the conception of an 'original sin' — i.e. the sin of Adam — in Christian theology.[18]

An important feature of the Greek mysteriosophy is that of man's birth and of this-worldly existence being a punishment (*timōria*, *kolasis*, *poina*), whose proper subject is the soul, buried in the body and tied to it.

Sometimes, the guilts of preceding lives (or even of the present one), or of 'ancestors' (*progonoi*), are compendiously hinted at;[19] consequently, the victims of misfortune are individuals[20] but also families[21] or political communities.[22] But far more characteristic is the mention of man being punished in (and by) this life; a statement which is often absolute and elusive, as if no further motivation or localization were needed or allowed.[23] As a rule, a general and indefinite phraseology adds to this impressive obscurity: '*some* punishments' (or rather 'a punishment for *some*thing': Philolaus, frg. 14 Timp.;[24] '*aliqua* scelera' (Cicero, l.c.); 'we all are under punishment', 'the soul is punished and our life is a punishment (*kolasis*) for *some* great guilt', says Iamblichus, Kern 8, quoting respectively the experts of initiations and the 'most ancient ones' (which, to some extent, amounts to the same); above all Plato, *Cratyl.* 400 c: 'the soul is punished for what it is punished, ... till having paid its due' (in relation to the body-prison doctrine of 'those with Orpheus') and Plato, *Phaedo*, 62 b: ἔν τινι φρουρᾷ ἐσμὲν οἱ ἄνϑρωποι.

In a golden *lamella* from Thurii the soul confesses to have 'given satisfaction (*poina*) for deeds unjust' (Kern 32 e 4), and a famous fragment from Pindar tells of men who have paid to Persephone 'the satisfaction (*poina*) of the ancient grief'.[25] Finally Plato, *Leges* 854 b: 'a (kind of) connaturate (*emphyomenos*) impulsion (*oistros...tis*) deriving from guilt old and inexpiate for men'; for which see also Olympiodorus (again *oistros*) and the famous 'ancient Titanic nature' of *Leges* III 701 c. Remember also the Pythagorean catechism quoted by Iamblichus: '... we came into the world in order to be punished ...; we shall be punished' (resp. Kern 232, *Vita Pyth.* 85).

This kind of thought is commonplace in Greek mysteriosophy; it can be traced from Presocratic philosophers (particularly Empedocles) and archaic Orphism and Pythagoreanism down to Plato, Neoplatonism and so-called 'Christian' gnosticism. (So, the Naassene treatise 'On Man', quoted by Hippolytus, *Refut.* V, 7,7; in this text, the terrestrial man is given a soul, in order that, by means of soul, this 'creature of the great celestial Anthropos' may suffer and be punished: again *kolasis*.[26] This speculation, says Hippolytus, is based on the *mystika* (i.e. pagan mysticism), not on the Holy Scripture. The symbols of this vicissitude of the soul and of life are actually in the Naassene treatise Adonis, Endymion, and Attis; though the reference to pagan mystery religion and philosophy is commonplace in Hippolytus: consider e.g. his identification between Empedoclean and gnostic conceptions of fall: cfr. ap. Emped., Diels B 115, quoted above and *Refut.* V, 20,4, relating to the Sethians).

We are faced here with the transcendental and dualistic character of 'previous sin' and its ontological foundations: the principle of Multiplicity, or Discord, or worldly Destiny, or planetarian Time.

Generally speaking, this kind of dualism implies a radical, connaturate split within the very roots of human existence, which accordingly is put into being by a corresponding split within the Primordial and sometimes Divine, that is by a previous, not-human, not terrestrial sin, — be it the evil deed of a divine, pleromatic entity, Sophia of Valentinianism, or Anthropos of the Poimandres, be it the corresponding selfish intervention and blasphematory pride of a gnostic or Promethean demiurge.[27]

In conclusion: the distinction between a previous sin, which is prehuman and dualistic, and an original sin in the sense of Christian theology is clear. This distinction is very important for the religio-historical understanding of gnosticism, and the connections between Gnosticism and Greek mysteriosophy. May I quote here Hans Jonas' statement: 'But note that (in Gnosticism) mankind is not responsible for its plight and for the necessity of divine intervention. There is no fall or original sin of Adam: where he is the first recipient of revelation (as is often the case), he is this not as transgressor but as victim — directly of archontic oppression, and ultimately of the primordial fall to which the world's existence and his own are due. Insofar as guilt is involved, it is not his but that of the Aeons who caused the disruption of the highest order; it is not human but divine, arising before, and not in creation. This difference from the Jewish and Christian position goes to the heart of the gnostic phenomenon. Among other things, it made Gnosticism unable to assimilate any serious meaning of the incarnation and the cross'.[28]

We can test this position with the example of the gnostic Basilides and his theory of the *hamartētikon*, the sinful quality, or better: the sinful inclination which exists in every man who experiences suffering, be he the most innocent.[29] This conception could be easily confronted with the Christian conception of original sin and its consequences; but the difference remains, given the fact that Basilides is unable to explain suffering without the idea of a sin which is previous to this life, — and this leads him to the conception of *metensōmatōsis*, conceived as an instrument of punishment for the evil deeds of previous lives of the same individual, or at least as a punishment for his *hamartētikon*, i.e. his tendency to sin. Basilides cannot accept the idea of the Suffering Just. To accept it would mean for him to be blasphemous against Providence. We see here an affinity of Basilides' theology with the Indian conception of *karma*, an affinity frequently observed by scholars. According to Basilides even the suffering martyr — nay the suffering Christ, so Clemens interprets Basilides' paradox, — does pay a guilt or a *hamartētikon* present in him:[30] a paradox obviously unacceptable from the point of view of Christian theology, a paradox depending upon the dualistic pre-comprehension of Basilides. According to this pre-comprehension there exists in man an evil, which is substance, an evil soul which is added to the soul of the sinner or of the man inclined to sin.

Having reached this conclusion, we would like to add that there were sometimes partial overlappings between the two conceptions, the previous sin and the original sin. Suffice it to think of Origenes and Origenian Fathers, with their conception of an original creation and a second creation; the latter implies, according to them, a connection between sin — a kind of previous sin — and the heavy corporeity, the sexual corporeity, of man. But this is a distinct issue which we cannot treat in the context of this limited presentation.[31]

NOTES:

1. See respectively U. Bianchi, ΔΙΟΣ ΑΙΣΑ. *Destino, uomini e divinita, nell' epos, nelle teogonie e nel culto dei Greci*, Roma 1953; id., *fatum* and *Giove* in the *Enciclopedia Virgiliana*, Roma 1985 ff.; id., *Zamān i Ohrmazd. Lo zoroastrismo nelle sue origini e nella sua essenza*, Torino 1958.
2. Author's *Selected Essays in Gnosticism, Dualism and Mysteriosophy*, Leiden 1978, pp. 159-207.
3. ΔΙΟΣ ΑΙΣΑ, cit., chapter One.
4. O. Kern, *Orphicorum fragmenta*, Berlin 1922, no. 32 c d e.
5. Op.cit. on n. 2, pp. 159-176.
6. ΔΙΟΣ ΑΙΣΑ, cit., chapter Two.
7. True, there is the question, here, of the initiatory 'vocabulary' of such a poem as the *Bacchae* of Euripides, and also of the *original* meaning of the distinction between *narthēkophoroi* and *bakchoi* mentioned by Plato, *Phaedo* 69 c, but in the interest of his own argumentation concerning the superiority of wisdom. This text should be studied in comparison with the distinction made by Diodoros IV, 3, 2 between the *parthenoi*, which carry the *thyrsos*, and the married women (*gynaikes*) whose ritual acting consists in θυσιάζειν, βακχεύειν, τὴν παρουσίαν ὑμνεῖν τοῦ Διονύσου. Doing so, they imitate those maenads 'who are said to have accompanied the god in ancient times'.
8. *Hymn. Hom. Cerer.* 479 ff.; Pindar, frg. 137 Schr.; Sophocl., frg. 753 N².
9. Aristoph., *Frogs* 154 ff. e 448 ff.
10. *Apud* Stob. IV, p. 1089 H. See our contribution to the *Mélanges* in honor of P. Boyancé, Rome 1974, pp. 73-77.
11. Istituto per la civiltà fenicia e punica, *Adonis*. Relazioni del Colloquio di Roma 22-23 maggio 1981, pp. 73-81.
12. Quoted by Plato, *Gorgias* 492 e.

13. 'Revue de l'histoire des religions' t. 170, 2 (1966), pp. 117-126 = *Selected Essays*, cit., pp. 177-186.
14. See the discussion between G. Quispel and H. Jonas in Hyatt (Ed.), *The Bible in Modern Scholarship*, New York 1967.
15. 'Rivista di storia e letteratura religiosa' 9, 1 (1973), pp. 3-16 = *Selected Essays*, cit., pp. 49-62, and *Il dualismo religioso*[2], Roma 1983, pp. 3-6.
16. 'Paideuma' 7 (1961), pp. 414-437 = *Selected Essays*, cit., pp. 126-150.
17. This was pertinently remarked by Dr. M.V. Cerutti in a Seminar on this topic.
18. *Supra*, n. 13.
19. *Veteres illi sive vates sive in sacris initiisque tradendis divinae mentis interpretes, qui nos ob aliqua scelera suscepta in vita superiore poenarum luendarum causa natos esse dixerunt* ..., Cicer., *Hortensius* frg. 88 Bait, Kern, *Orphicorum fragmenta* 8, cfr. 31 (3rd cent.B.C.) and 232. See also Proclus' *Hymn to the Muses* and Kern, 229 f.
20. Plat., *Resp.* II 364 b c, 366 a b and *Phaedr.* 244 d; also Pausan. IX, 30, 4 (Kern, *test.* 93).
21. See the preceding note.
22. *Resp.* II 364 e, cfr. 366 a b.
23 See *infra*.
24. διά τινας τιμωρίας. The text reminds us of that of the *Hortensius*. It quotes 'the ancient *theologoi* and *manties*'.
25. Ap. Plat., *Meno* 81 b.
26. Cfr. also Nag Hammadi's *Apoc Adam.* 77, 18.
27. See n. 16.
28. In U. Bianchi (Ed.), *The Origins of Gnosticism*, Leiden 1967 (1970[2]), p. 98 f.
29. *Apud* Clem. Al., *Strom.* IV, 8, 81-83.
30. But this interpretation by Clemens seems wrong, according to M. Simonetti, *Testi gnostici cristiani*, Bari 1970, p. 94 n. 7.
31. See for this U. Bianchi (Ed.), *Archè e telos. L'antropologia di Origene* ..., Milano 1979 (SPM 12).

THE MYTH OF ATTIS: STRUCTURE AND MYSTERIOSOPHY

by Jørgen Podemann Sørensen

One of the great merits of our guest is to have brought the comparative insights of the history and ethnology of religions into the field of hellenistic studies. The following contribution may perhaps be seen as a few steps along the same line, since the myth of Attis will be examined in the light of certain insights gained through the study of myth in non-literate societies. I shall not present an orthodox Levi-Straussean or Greimassian analysis of the myth of Attis, but I share with these gentlemen the opinion that structural analysis will reveal the central concerns of a myth. My project is to examine the structure of the Attis myth in Arnobius[1] in an attempt to uncover its essential concerns and then to ask, in a general way, for possible connections between this myth and hellenistic mysteriosophy.

The choice of Arnobius' version of the Attis myth, however, will already need some justification. First, when we ask for possible connections with mystery cult and mysteriosophy, only the so-called pessinuntian versions will be immediately relevant. Second, of all the pessinuntian versions, Arnobius is by far the most comprehensive one, comprising as it does all the essential features of the other versions. Except for the allegedly Phrygian version of Diodorus,[2] which differs from all other versions, Arnobius' is the only one that looks like a myth narrated in full. It has all the oddities, absurdities and obscenities that a defender of Christianity might conceivably want; a structuralist, I believe, would become enthusiastic about exactly the same qualities. And, thirdly, it is the only version to connect the Attis myth with a primeval sequence of events, thus providing information about the mythological context of Attis. One disadvantage of the Arnobian myth, however, is that there is a great range of possibilities as to the date of this version. What can be stated with certainty is that the myth was known in the beginning of the 4th century when Arnobius wrote, and that most of it may go back as far as the 3rd century B.C., if the theologian Thimotheus, whom Arnobius cites as his main source, be the eumolpid Timotheos who was instrumental in fashioning the Serapis cult under Ptolemy I.[3] This disadvantage, however, it shares with other versions: we can date the text, not the tradition.

At this point it will be useful, I believe, to recall the main features of Arnobius' version of the Attis myth: At its outset stands Agdus, a rock in the Phrygian wasteland, from which Deucalion and Pyrrha threw stones into the void later to be populated by men. It was on this occasion, Arnobius says, that the Great Mother of the Gods originated. Asleep or resting on the rock she was desired by voluptuous Juppiter. It is not clear whether rape or seduction was intended, but anyway Juppiter did not succeed in his attempts, but poured his semen on the rock. Agdus conceived and in due time gave birth to Agdestis, a wild and extremely libidinous being of both sexes. His very wildness and voluptuousness seemed dangerous to the gods, and they decided to have him tempered and civilized. With this end in view, Liber changed Agdestis' drinking water into wine and — when he was drunk and safely asleep — tied his male parts to a trunk in the forest. The plan worked; when Agdestis woke and rose to his feet, he bereaved himself of those same parts and ceased to be a man.

The soil conceived with the blood running from his wound, and a pomegranate with fruits was born. Nana, daughter of the river-god Sangarius, picked one, put it in her lap, and became pregnant. Ashamed of such premarital pregnancy her father shut her up to let her starve, but the Great Mother kept her alive, discretely nourishing her with apples.

The child, Attis, is born, but Sangarius orders him to be exposed. He is nourished, however, 'with a he-goat's milk' and grows up to be a beauty that exceeds human measure. Both the Great Mother and Agdestis love him, and Agdestis becomes the companion of Attis, who profits from his strength and skill in hunting in the woodlands of Phrygia. At some time Attis must have been in Pessinus on his own and established certain connections with urban civilization there, for we are told that he boasted of his good bag, which was really due to the hunting skill of Agdestis. But once again wine has a role to play: Attis gets drunk and betrays that the great hunter is not himself, but Agdestis, who loves him.

Midas, the king of Pessinus, wants Attis to give up such improper companionship and marry his own daughter. The wedding is decided and the town is closed to avoid any disturbance of the ceremony. But the Great Mother of the Gods knew that Attis would only be safe among men if he did not marry. Accordingly she went into the closed town, lifting the town walls with her head. Agdestis, stung into fury by the loss of Attis and the marriage, seems to have taken this opportunity to enter the town and the wedding party. He inspires all the guests with fury and madness, probably by means of flute-playing; for we are told later that he carried a reed pipe. There is a crux in the text at this point, but we gather that the Phrygians shriek with horror. A daughter of Gallus'[4] concubine cuts off her breasts, and Attis himself, full of mad frenzy, rushes out and under a pine-tree cuts off his male parts.

Attis dies from the loss of blood. His male parts are wrapped in his clothes and buried by the Great Mother. From his blood the violet springs up. His bride covers his breast with soft wool, sheds tears with Agdestis and takes her own life. Her blood in turn becomes purple violets. She is buried by the Mother and an almond grows from the grave.

Now the Mother of the Gods takes the pine tree to her cave, and together with Agdestis she laments Attis there, beating and wounding her breast. Later Agdestis asks Juppiter to revive Attis, but this is impossible. Juppiter is, however, able to grant that Attis' body should never decay, that his hair should ever grow, and that the smallest of his fingers alone should be able to move forever. Agdestis now consecrates the body and establishes a mortuary cult of Attis with annual rites.

I must apologize for this long paraphrase, but since I am going to deal with the structure apparent in the very redundancy of the myth, I could not even omit those features that are usually left untranslated. The myth displays a number of themes which recur in an inverted form. In the beginning, divine or human life issues from not-life, i.e. stone; towards the end, vegetal life originates from death. In the beginning, seduction or rape is prevented, and in the end matrimony is prevented. Likewise Agdestis is a wild hermaphrodite, engendered by a rock and a male, Attis a civilized male, son of a woman and a pomegranate. Wine is used to prevent Agdestis from discovering what is going on, and wine makes Attis reveal everything. Agdestis is emasculated in order to temper and civilize this wild being, Attis emasculates himself as a result of wild frenzy. Nana is shut up to starve, but survives on vegetal food,

Attis is exposed, but survives on animal nourishment. As for Nana, her death is prevented and birth is the result; as for Attis, procreation is prevented, death the result.

These preliminary observations show that themes like life and death, male and female, wildness and civilization, vegetal and human procreation, are among the building stones of the myth. They also leave the impression that the myth may be divided into two symmetrical parts, in which the themes of the first part recur in an inverted form in the second part. We shall now examine in greater detail and more systematically how the themes are arranged in the myth.

The myth may be seen as a kind of trial and error process, as a series of experiments. The first theme is life and not-life, divine or human life issuing from stone. This pair of opposites is then replaced by a weaker opposition, that between male and female. This theme is continuous with the preceding one; the male-female relationship is highly relevant to the creation or procreation theme, and furthermore the male, Juppiter, is seen as the active part, whereas the female, the Great Mother, seems rather inert and therefore closer to not-life in the first theme. This aspect, the wild, voluptuous Juppiter and the chaste mother resisting his attempts, already points forward to the next binary opposition, that between wild and civilized. Agdestis mediates the male-female opposition because he is both male and female, and since he is the offspring of a male, Juppiter, and a lifeless substance, the rock, he may also be considered a mediator of the opposition involved in the first two themes: life from lifeless stone vs. life from male-female union. But the ferocity of Agdestis introduces a new opposition: wildness vs. civilization. At this stage, civilization is represented by the council of the gods anxiously deliberating how to civilize the savage hermaphrodite. The means to temper him is emasculation, but this in turn gives rise to new experiments with life and procreation.

From soil and blood a pomegranate springs up, and thus vegetal life is begotten by a still more neutral pair: the soil is not as lifeless as stone, and blood is not necessarily male or female. When Nana is impregnated by the pomegranate the opposition between the two parts in the procreative process is still weaker because both are definitely alive. But the opposition between human or divine civilization and wild nature is still present and in fact it is strengthened anew. Obviously river-god society resists pre-marital sex, for the pregnancy of Nana is considered a scandal, and when Attis is born he is exposed. Civilization is closed to Attis, and he is left to the wild woodlands of Phrygia.

But Attis certainly is a mediator: he is born of a civilized woman, but of vegetal descent, and he is reared in wild nature where he is nourished on a he-goat's milk. He is full of contradictions and paradoxes, but with immense potentialities as a mediator of the opposed themes of the myth. For some time he tries to be both wild and civilized, but is catched by civilization. When Attis enters civilization and is going to marry the daughter of the king of Pessinus, the two basic oppositions are displayed at full strength: wildness and civilization, male and female. In order to 'survive' as a mediator, Attis must go mad, become wild in civilized surroundings, and above all, he must become *neither* male *nor* female. He dies in this very process, but as dead he is able to mediate other basic oppositions in the myth: life vs. not-life and vegetal vs. animal or human life. Vegetals spring from his blood and the strange condition of his dead body recalls such concepts as not-life, at earlier stages represented by stone, vegetal growth, and movement as a characteristic of animal and human life.

The myth ends up with a perfect mediation of the horizontal oppositions that it displays. But displaying these opposed themes the myth also moves vertically through a number of stages. The first is primeval time, where wildness and civilization are not clearly separated. Only great gods as the Mother and Juppiter occur at this stage. On the next level the wildness vs. civilization theme is very clear: the council of the gods is deliberating how to temper, or civilize, wild Agdestis. It is the organized community of the gods standing against a ferocious being. — The next stage might be called the river-god level; and here the problem is nearly reduced to a question of bourgeois morality: The non-marital pregnancy of Nana is unacceptable to river-god society.

The following events take place on a human level, and their drastic outcome is due to an encounter between wildness and urban civilization. The intrusion of wildness into the closed town and the outbreak of madness at the wedding party are exactly what produces a full mediation. This mediation, however, secures a connection between the human and the primeval or divine level. Attis is not only a mediator of the horizontal oppositions throughout the myth, but uniting all these opposed themes he also represents primeval unity on the human level. When the dead Attis unites life and not-life, this may be seen as a return to the primeval level, where life issued from stone. And when an end is put to sexual reproduction this may likewise be seen as a return to that stage, where life comes from stone and where the male-female relation is not yet relevant to the creation of life.

The process of the myth is in a way circular. The last stage to a very large degree agrees with the first, and this agreement is brought about by the emasculation and death of Attis. It may be worth while to add that it is these events that bring the Great Mother 'down to Earth', where she laments Attis. In the other parts of the myth she has always been working behind the stage.

One of the tasks carried out by this myth is clearly to account for the ritual competence of the priests of the Great Mother: by imitating the frenzy and emasculation of Attis they are able to enter into communication with the divine. By becoming wild in civilized surroundings and by becoming *neither* male *nor* female they render themselves primeval in the sense of the myth.

The question about a possible basis for hellenistic mysteriosophy in the Attis myth as told by Arnobius may be put in a quite general way. I believe to have demonstrated that the Arnobius version is not dualistic. It is full of binary oppositions, but there are not, as far as I see, two single principles at work throughout this myth. How then, could it be the basis of mysteriosophy?

The classical paradigm to account for both the continuity and the discontinuity of pre-hellenistic cults and mystery religions is the dying and resurrecting god reflecting or representing the vegetational cycle. In pre-hellenistic cults the vegetational cycle, which is of immediate importance in an agricultural society, would have been stressed, whereas hellenistic man would have found a prototype for his individual salvation in the dying and resurrecting god. But already Nilsson[5] pointed out that this paradigm does not seem to be valid in the case of Attis. Except for the vague generalizations of Firmicus Maternus[6] there is no textual evidence for a resurrection of Attis, and nowhere else does he represent vegetation or the vegetational cycle. In the myth we just surveyed, although vegetation is important, Attis cannot be said to represent it or to be the cause or model of its cycle.

Yet it is easy — still generally speaking — to see what hellenistic man might find attractive or relevant to salvation in this myth. As the vast majority of myths, it accounts for the continuity and discontinuity of primeval time and present time, of divine and human. What is peculiar about it is that access to the divine is reached through what might be termed a process of emancipation from human society and from the general human condition. Here lies the connecting point between this myth and hellenistic mysteriosophy. That the emancipation process was also destructive to the human body could only strengthen dualist interest in the myth.

Now, to be less general and more specific, there is at least one mysteriosophic interpretation of the myth that fixes its attention exactly at this point: That of Sallustius the Neoplatonic in his delightful little treatise 'On the gods and the world'.[7] To make a dualist myth of the myth of Attis, Sallustius has to employ allegoric interpretation. But strangely enough, his interpretation of the Attis myth is less addicted to allegoric licence than any of his other interpretations. There was one point in the myth, to which he could do justice in another way, namely the emancipation process. He sees Attis who is about to marry as representing the human condition. We are all about to marry, we are tempted by this world of becoming and perishableness. What we should do is to detach ourselves from it and return to the divine origin.

This single example, I believe, will show for the possibility of a basis for mysteriosophy in the myth, also as understood by structural analysis. We may account for both the meaning of the myth and its continuity and discontinuity with hellenistic mysteriosophy without the resurrection of Attis.

At last I must regret that I had to keep straight to the line of my own argument and could not discuss the work of numerous collegues. But I want at least to state my profound agreement with professor Bianchi and his pupils that certain analogies with mysteriosophic speculation exist in pre-mysteriosophic material. What I have tried to show is that in the Attis myth of Arnobius, such analogies are found in mythical structure.

NOTES:

1. Arnobius, *adverersus nationes*, V, 5-7.
2. Diodorus Siculus, III, 58-59.
3. Cf. Nilsson, M.P.: *Geschichte der griechischen Religion*; Bd. 2, München 1961, p. 641.
4. Probably a new name for the king of Pessinus, due to contamination of different traditions. Cf. Hepding, H.: *Attis, seine Mythen und sein Kult*. Giessen 1903, p. 109, n. 3.
5. Nilsson, *op.cit*, p. 649 sq.
6. *De errore profanarum religionum*, 3.
7. Ch. IV. – Cf. Sallustios: *Des dieux et du monde*. Ed. G. Rochefort. Paris 1961.

THE MEANING OF ROMAN MITHRAISM

by Per Bilde

1. Introduction

The aim of this essay is to make yet another attempt to penetrate into the essential religious content of the Mysteries of Mithras in Roman times.[1] This attempt will not be done by presenting new source-material or new interpretations of this or that well known detail in our archaeological, iconographical and literary sources. Nor is it my primary concern to answer any of the classical questions in the various departments of Mithraic Studies. Instead, after a brief survey of the present situation in Mithraic research, I will try to pose some new questions and to discuss holistically some new combinations of a few fundamental issues.

I have chosen the two most essential features in Mithraism: first, the indispensable cultic picture, Mithras Tauroctonos, and secondly, the cultic edifice itself, the mithraeum. These two elements are discussed both separately and in combination in this paper, and on this background, I propose to consider once again the issue of the religious content and meaning of the Mysteries of Mithras.

Accordingly, this article does not contribute towards the more specific problems of the origin and genesis of Mithraism, of the creation, on some Iranian and Hellenistic basis, of the Roman mysteries, of their possible religio-historical development, of the geographical and socio-economic development and distribution of the religion, of the interpretation of the seven Mithraic grades, and the initiations and trials connected in all probability with the seven grades, of the astrological, magical, or even gnostic aspects of the Mysteries of Mithras, or of others of the numerous important questions still under discussion in Mithraic studies. Despite remarkable progress in interpreting Mithraism in recent years, the discussion of these essential

The point of departure has to be taken in the center of the religion, i.e. in Mithras, which again, first and foremost, is a matter of understanding correctly the meaning of the central bull-slaying act, and secondly, the connexion between this act and the ritual and worship in the Mithraic sanctuary.

3. Mithras Tauroctonos

The most crucial question in Mithraic studies is that of the significance of the bull-slaying scene which is the most frequent in Mithraic art. Some kind of figuration of it seems to have adorned every single mithraeum, where it is situated in a central position as the most important part of the sanctuary. Turcan has rightly compared the image of the bull-slaying scene with the crucifix in the Christian churches.[23]

However obvious it is that the bull-slaying scene is the central cultic decoration in the mithraeum and represents the fundamental event in Roman Mithraism, it is just as uncertain what the meaning of this essential act is. In the first place, it is an astonishing fact that this scene is not even mentioned once in our literary sources.[24] In Porphyrios we learn, that 'the moon is the bull'.[25] And in Statius we read about Mithras fighting the obstinate bull, which is not willing to follow him.[26] However, the bull-slaying scene as such — Mithras killing the bull and all the consequences that follow from this act — is not referred to by Statius either.[27] What Statius is in fact talking about, may be the scene of Mithras carrying the bull away on his shoulders at an earlier stage of the mythological story.[28] Or perhaps it is a scene which is not known from the epigraphical sources, but which may be assumed to exist in the myth between Mithras' catching and carrying away the bull, on the one hand, and his killing it, on the other. None of the remaining literary sources even mentions the bull. Consequently, it has to be noted as a fact, that the decisive bull-slaying scene is not referred to in the existing literary sources. The reason for this state of affairs could be the fact that our sources are few, fragmentary, and rather biased. But in comparison with the situation regarding other mystery religions, the existing collection of the literary sources to Roman Mithraism cannot be considered small, just as they are not more biased than sources to other religions either. And our sources are not so fragmentary and unrepresentative, that they fail to mention several times a number of other important features such as the cave, the seven grades, the trials, the religion's

Persian character, the cultic images in the mithraea, etc. It therefore remains a mystery, that our comparatively numerous sources do not mention the fundamental event of Roman Mithraism. And this mystery has to be taken seriously into account when critically estimating the value of these sources.

The classical interpretation of the bull-slaying scene is that of Cumont, who was followed by Vermaseren and many others.[29] According to Cumont, Mithras unwillingly obeyed the command of the Sun God and thus killed or rather sacrificed the bull. And after the sacrifice followed the great miracle, as all kinds of good plants grew out of the slaughtered animal. But the evil forces let loose their unclean beasts, the snake and the scorpion, on the bull. In vain, however. Life triumphed in spite of its opponents. By this act Mithras thus created life and fertility.

This classical interpretation is not completely satisfactory. It stands isolated as a fragmentary torso, which has not been brought into connexion with the Mithraic myth and ritual as a whole.[30] Furthermore, the ideas of Mithras being 'unwilling' and of the snake and the scorpion being 'evil' animals have rightly been criticized.[31]

A modern view is the Platonizing and Neo-Pythagorizing dualistic one advocated most effectively by Merkelbach.[32] Using primarily Polybios (Eubulos and Pallas) and Origin (Celsus) as sources, Merkelbach interprets Mithraism as a dualistic Hellenistic religion influenced heavily by Orphicism, Platonism and Neo-Pythagorism. On the basis of these texts, Merkelbach (and others) understand the seven grades and the seven gates on the Ostian mosaic from the 'Mitreo delle sette porte'[33] in connexion with the seven planets and planetary spheres. This interpretation, accordingly, emphasizes the astrological character of Mithraism and is viewing the religion as a typical Hellenistic religion of salvation. The aim is the salvation of the individual soul from the corporeal body and the material world. The point in the Mithraic initiation and salvation is thus assumed to be the journey of the soul, under the guidance of Mithras, from this world up through the seven planetary spheres to its original heavenly home beyond the stars. In this way, Mithraism is interpreted as being close both to the other mystery religions and to Gnosticism.[34] The Platonizing interpretation has been strongly opposed by Turcan, who has argued, that the literary sources in question are not genuine expressions of the Mysteries of Mithras, but rather represent Neo-Platonic and Neo-Pythagorean reinterpretations of an otherwise non-dualistic Mithraic religion.[35]

It may be added to Turcan's observations, that it seems difficult, if not impossible, to relate this Platonizing interpretation to the central bull-slaying scene in a natural way: Where is the cosmological and anthropological dualism to be found? Where are we confronted with the homeless human soul? How does Mithras appear as a psychopompos? It is not possible to answer these questions positively without allowing for major transformations in the history of Mithraism or for fairly artificial and arbitrary reinterpretations of the bull-slaying scene.[36]

Concerning the interpretation of Merkelbach and his followers, the central scene of the bull-slaying is not immediately and naturally understandable, a fact that is of no advantage methodologically. From a methodological point of view, it must be a requirement, that the bull-slaying scene is understood in a way which for the adherents of and the participants in the cult may be considered natural and easily understood. We must assume that this scene was intuitively understood as *the* central scene in which the decisive act was accomplished by Mithras to the obvious benefit of his followers. Furthermore, our point of departure has to be taken in the Roman archaeological material and not in the Iranian (as Cumont and Campbell) or in the later, secondary literary sources (as Merkelbach).[37] Let us then take one more look at the bull-slaying scene and consider each single feature of it together with the scene as a whole.

Mithras developed from the earlier Indian and Iranian gods (Mitra/Mithra) of light, justice, friendship, contract, oath etc.[38] Mithras was related to, if not identified with, the Sun God from the beginning.[39] In the Roman Mysteries of Mithras, we find the same ambiguity. On the one hand, Mithras is closely connected with the sun, as Sol seems to be the originator of the bull-slaying through the raven as intermediary. Mithras, on the other hand, seems to be identified with the sun: In some cases he is pictured with a torch, especially when portrayed as Mithras 'Saxigenus'.[40] In a few other representations, he is shown with a nimbus.[41] In yet another group, we see Mithras as being the superior master of the sun.[42] Further, Mithras' most common title is, as we know, *Sol Invictus*.[43] Consequently, not only in the religion's earlier stages but especially and with great emphasis in Roman Mithraism, Mithras is closely associated with the sun and light.

Both in the literary sources, as we have seen, and in Mithraic art, the bull is identified with the moon.[44] In several representations of the bull-slaying scene, the bull's shape closely resembles that of the new moon.[45] Similarly, some pictures show the bull in the moon's boat.[46] The intimate connexion, therefore, between the bull and the moon cannot be disputed.[47] And the moon is related to night and darkness just as Mithras is connected with light and day.

According to Cumont and others, the bull-slaying act is a sacrifice. This view has been questioned by Will, who has proposed an alternative interpretation of the act as a victory after a fight. Will emphasizes, that the representations stylistically express the triumphant victor and not the sacrificing priest.[48] Will's view corresponds well with the text of Statius, who, as we have seen, describes Mithras as *fighting* the recalcitrant bull. This is the point in the mythological story as well. In all reconstructions, the myth tells the story of Mithras pursuing, fighting, and killing the bull. The bull-slaying act, then, may well refer to the sun and the light defeating the moon and the darkness.

This interpretation seems to be confirmed by the two accompanying figures, Cautes and Cautopates. With the raised and the lowered torch they appear to refer to the same reality of light being lit and spread, and light being extinguished.[49]

Finally, the same phenomenon seems to be represented in Sol and Luna, who in numerous pictures are either portrayed as busts in medallions or in full person in their carts.[50] This fact may be taken as yet another sign of the importance in the bull-slaying scene of the duality day-night/light-darkness. Consequently, the fundamental opponents, light and darkness, and, correspondingly, life and death, seem to play an essential role in the bull-slaying scenery.

To make further progress in our interpretation, we turn to the other accompanying figures, the animals and the surrounding vegetation. The dog and the snake are shown as licking the blood of the slain bull. The scorpion seems to go for its testicles and its semen. Thus the bull appears to be giving life to the animal world.[51] The same seems to be true for the plants. Ears of corn shoot out of the dying bull's tail and, in some cases, from its wound in the neck as well.[52] And in a number of cases, blossoming and fruit-bearing trees are indicated besides or above the central bull-slaying scene.[53]

In sum, the bull-slaying scene seems to express the sun defeating the moon, light being victorious over darkness, and life prevailing over death. It is a fundamental and simple idea which allows for numerous literal and figurative interpretations. However, in the context of the bull-slaying scene, a rather literal and unsophisticated understanding seems to be dominating.[54]

4. The mithraeum

Is it possible for us to put our observations to a test? Once again, it is advisable to stick to the most fundamental facts and features in Roman Mithraism and ask for their mutual relations which was the reason for taking our starting point in the bull-slaying scene. Following the same line of thought, we now turn to the mithraeum, the characteristic sanctuary of the Roman Mysteries of Mithras.[55]

The mithraeum is in fact an outstanding and unique type of sanctuary, not only in the Greco-Roman world. All over the Roman Empire the mithraeum follows the same outline and pattern. It is always designed and constructed as a cave or a grotto. Its dimensions are modest, its ceiling is vaulted, and its atmosphere dark and dim. The whole arrangement is determined by one focal point, the bull-slaying scene, which is represented either in painting, in bas-relief, or in sculpture. The image is placed in a cultniche often raised a few steps on a sort of bema.

Mithras Tauroctonos, thus, is the navel of the mithraeum. Further, the bull-slaying act itself takes place in a cave.[56] And in the mithraeum, its representation is placed in a little cave, the cultniche, which, in turn, is constructed in a cave or a cave-like edifice, the mithraeum.[57] Both the mythological act and the Mithraic ritual, accordingly, take place in the same surroundings and context, the dark cave, or grotto.

Finally, the same is the case for another important feature in Mithraic art: the meal eaten in common by Mithras and the Sun God.[58] According to Vermaseren, this scene is the second most common in Mithraic iconography.[59] It was imagined in all probability to have taken place after Mithras killed the bull, since the dead bull is used as a table for their common meal. Mithras and the Sun God are the central figures. In a cave, they are sitting at the bull-table, and they are being served by masked 'ravens' and 'lions'.

There seems to exist a connexion between these different cave-scenes, and it may be wise to incorporate them in our interpretation as well.[60] This observation indicates that the mithraeum as a whole is to be considered as the scene of a meal. And this actually seems to have been the case. The two parallel benches must surely be eating places where the participants in a ritual meal would be lying, eating a meal while at the same time being able to look at and comtemplate the fundamental mythological scenes: the bull-slaying and the original meal. The mithraeum is thus first and foremost to be understood as a triclinium.[61] This interpretation finds some support in our literary sources. Justin mentions the eating of bread and the drinking of water,[62] this act being in his interpretation a diabolic imitation of the Christian Eucharist. And Tertullian writes that the Devil in his 'pagan mysteries' — his remark is general, and not specifically referring to Mithraism — both baptize some and 'celebrates the presentation of bread'.[63] Accordingly, our literary sources, despite their biased and fragmentary nature, confirm that a meal constituted an important part of the Mithraic ritual, a meal with a status allowing for comparison with the Christian Eucharist. In addition to the outline of the mithraeum and the allusions in the literary sources, reference may finally be made to the many bones of animals found in and around the mithraea, a fact which can be interpreted as indicating that cultic meals played an important role in Roman Mithraism.[64]

It may be assumed, then, that the mithraeum was imagined as a duplicate of the primordial cave, which, in turn, seems to have represented the world or the universe.[65] Further, we feel entitled to suppose, that the Mithraic ritual consisted primarily of a cultic meal that reiterated the mythical meal following Mithras' slaying of the bull.[66]

5. Conclusions

Our discussion and reflexions point to the assumption that a sacramental meal constituted the heart of Roman Mithraism.[67] The mithraeum itself was obviously designed as a dining hall, and Mithraic worship seems to have concentrated on a ritual reiteration of the mythological meal which was supposed to have followed Mithras' fundamental slaying of the bull. The killing of the bull, according to the figurative representations of Mithras Tauroctonos, gave life to fauna and flora. And in the mythological meal which followed, the bull appears to have been the same source of life for Mithras and the Sun God. The mithraeum is obviously layed out and constructed as the same sort of cave as the mythological one, in which both the bull-slaying and the prototypical meal took place. This fact, combined with the observation, that the mithraeum is designed as a dining hall, indicate the conclusion, that essentially the same event was supposed to take place in myth and in ritual.

The idea of the sacramental meal, according to our observations, is as simple as the promotion of life, light and vitality. Through the victory over and the killing of the bull, and through the sacramental meal on the defeated animal afterwards, it seems that life and light were thought to be secured. In the first place, the living world, the animals and the vegetation received life through Mithras' act. But in reality, this also holds true for the world, the cosmos, and the universe as a whole. At least, this is a likely conclusion when we take into consideration the astrological figures in the representations of the bull-slaying scene. The idea of the cave as a symbol of the world point in the same direction. Further, in the mythological meal, this idea seems to have been realized for the gods — Mithras and the Sun God — as well. And, as the difference between gods and humans is thought neither in Iran nor in the Greco-Roman world to be absolute and categorical, this included in principle human beings as well.[68] In the Mithraic cult-meal, finally, all the beneficial effects of the mythlogical act appear to have been transferred to the participants in the ritual.

According to this analysis, Mithras is primarily understood as a victorious god of life and light. By means of his fundamental act, he is victorious over death and darkness, night and winter, drought and barrenness.[69] He is *Sol Invictus* in all the senses of the title. In a dark cave and a dark (and threatened) world, Mithras brings life and light, so that the world becomes the living and friendly cosmos.

An amazing corollary to this line of thought is the assertion, that the Mysteries of Mithras were not a usual mystery religion of the so-called pessimistic, dualistic, soteriological type. Mithras is not a dying and rising god, but a living, vital, and triumphant figure.[70] His function is not to save the spiritual human soul out of its captivity in a material body and world. The point in Mithraic soteriology is not the journey of the soul from the body and this world up through the seven spheres to the realm of the eternal fixed stars. This type of interpretation of Roman Mithraism appears to be forced and unnatural. The Mysteries of Mithras are not an individualistic but rather a collective religion. Mithras is saving man and the world in bringing life, light, fertility, and order. His salvation is vitalization. The Mysteries of Mithras are then an optimistic, this-worldly and monistic religion.[71]

This conclusion corresponds well with the description of the socio-economic status of the followers of Mithras, as we have seen earlier in this essay.[72] The community of Mithras seems to have been dominated by the stronger layers of the Roman society, of groups that both in public administration (the army, the fiscus, the customs etc.)

and in private enterprise on the one hand supported and on the other benefited from the existing social order. The participants in the Mysteries of Mithras seem to have felt well at home in this world and in the Roman Empire. And their position and attitude correspond surprisingly well with the interpretation of the religious contents of Roman Mithraism given above.

Whether the Mysteries of Mithras in their later stages underwent a secondary dualistic, Platonizing, and Neo-Pythagorizing reinterpretation, may still remain an open question. At least, some of our sources (Origin and Porphyr) understood and interpreted that religion along these lines. But this is not the meaning of Roman Mithraism as it may be reconstructed on the basis of the central features of Mithraic archaeology and iconography.

Our conclusions have not been reached through an analysis of the existing literary sources. As we have seen, none of these refer to the fundamental bull-slaying scene. Correspondingly, only a few of them refer to the Mithraic cultic meal, and when they do, it is in an allusive and rather noninformative way. It has to be noted, therefore, as one of our conclusions, that there is a considerable gap between the reality of Roman Mithraism, as it may be reconstructed on the basis of the archaeological and iconographical sources, and the literary evidence. This fact must be considered as an additional proof of the problematic nature of the literary sources.

Our final remark will necessarily be methodological. When it comes to the interpretation of the essential religious contents of Roman Mithraism, the appropriate method is a 'centralistic', holistic, and contextual one: What did this religion, according to its own sources, mean to its followers at the peak of its existence? In order to answer this question, we have to look for the central and essential features of the Mysteries of Mithras in Roman times. We maintain that these were the mithraeum itself and the fundamental bull-slaying scene. Finally, taking our point of departure in these two central features, we have attempted to combine these holistically and to interpret them in the context of other essential features in our sources.

NOTES:

1. In general, the reader is referred to the comprehensive works of Cumont (1896-1899 and [5]1981), Campbell, Harsberg, Merkelbach, Schwertheim, Turcan (1981), and Vermaseren (1963). These and other investigations referred to in this essay are listed in the appended bibliography.
2. No general survey of Mithraic research is presented in Cumont ([5]1981), Campbell, Harsberg, Merkelbach, Turcan (1981) or Vermaseren (1963). Further, I am aware of no essay covering this requirement, although some elements of an outline of modern research are given in Gordon (1973) and Hinnells (1971, in reviewing Campbell).
3. As to publication and registration, cf. primarily Cumont (1896-1899), Vermaseren (1956-1960), and Vermaseren (1971-1982).
4. Among recent scholars, Campbell and Turcan have in several respects returned to the positions of Cumont.
5. Cf. Cumont, [5]1981, pp. 1-11; Lommel, pp. 207-211; Merkelbach, pp. 9-39; Schwertheim, pp. 9-13; Turcan, 1981, pp. 5-11, and Vermaseren, 1963, pp. 13-18.
6. Cf. Beskow; Cumont, [5]1981, pp. 29-75; Merkelbach, pp. 43-72 and 146-153; Schwertheim, pp. 19-29; Turcan, 1981, pp. 24-37, and Vermaseren, 1963, pp. 30-36.
7. Cf. especially Gordon (1972); Harsberg, pp. 46-48; Merkelbach, pp. VIII, 30 and 153 ff.; Turcan, 1981, pp. 31 ff., and Will, pp. 534-536.
8. Cf. Gordon, 1972, pp. 95 and 102 ff.; Merkelbach, pp. 30, 40 and 153-173; Turcan, 1981, p. 114, and Will, pp. 534-536.
9. Cf. Cumont, [5]1981, pp. 10-28; Nock, p. 109; Schwertheim, pp. 13-18; Turcan, 1981, pp. 16-23, and Vermaseren, 1963, pp. 18-26.
10. Such as supposed by Wikander.
11. Rome has been suggested by Merkelbach who, elaborating on the idea of Nilsson, pp. 675-676, assume that Roman Mithraism has been created in Rome by a 'religious genius', cf. *op.cit.*, pp. 49, 76-77, 109 and 161. According to Speidel, the origins of the mysteries of Mithras is to be found in the Greek hero Orion.
12. E.g. Schwertheim, pp. 13-18, and Turcan, 1981, pp. 16-23.
13. Primarily on the basis of Plutarch, *Pompeius* 24, this has been assumed by e.g. Campbell, p. 179; Vermaseren, 1963, pp. 22, 24 and 28-30, and Will, pp. 529-534.
14. Cf. primarily Merkelbach, pp. 45 and 146-149.
15. Cf. Campbell, pp. 291-316; Cumont, [5]1981, pp. 138-148; Merkelbach, pp. 77 ff. and 86 ff.; Turcan, 1981, pp. 88-91, and Vermaseren, 1963, pp. 138-153.
16. In spite of the attempts of Merkelbach.
17. It is doubtful whether animal sacrifices were performed in Roman Mithraism, but there can be little doubt that meals were eaten in the caves. In a number of places pits filled by animal bones have been found, cf. Kane, p. 350, and Schwertheim, p. 57. And in a mithraeum in Riegel in Germany,

excavations have unearthed a stock of apparently cultic tabelware, cf. Merkelbach, p. 140, and Schwertheim, pp. 57 and 73.
18. This assumption is based on the texts of Gregor and Nonnus and the wall-paintings uncovered in the mithraeum of Santa Maria Vetere in Capua, cf. Merkelbach, pp. 85-86 and 136-140.
19. Cf. Cumont, [5]1981, pp. 10-11 and 26. Speidel accepts that there is a strong astrological element in Roman Mithraism, but he maintains that this element is Greek, and not Babylonian.
20. This is the fundamental assumption of Merkelbach, cf. *op.cit.*, pp. VII-VIII, 76, 84 ff., 109, 200, 230 ff. etc. Turcan, 1981, p. 16, as well is critical of Cumont's thesis although he is not following Merkelbach either.
21. So e.g. Cumont, [5]1981, pp. 19, 22, 26, 84 ff., 95 ff. and 164 ff.; Hinnells, 1975, pp. 309 and 312; Lincoln, pp. 506 ff.; Nock, pp. 111 and 113, and Vermaseren, 1963, p. 111.
22. Cf. e.g. Harsberg, p. 17; Merkelbach, p. VIII etc.; Speidel, pp. 43-45, and Wikander, pp. 21 ff. and 40. Campbell and Turcan are stressing the importance of both elements.
23. Cf. Turcan, 1981, p. 72.
24. This fact is noted by Vermaseren, 1963, p. 68, as well.
25. *De antro nympharum* 18, quoted from Cumont, 1896, p. 40: '... ⟨καὶ⟩ ἐπεὶ ταῦρος μὲν σελήνη ⟨καὶ ὕψωμα σελήνης ὁ ταῦρος ...'
26. *Thebais* I, 717-720, quoted from Cumont, 1896, p. 46: '... *seu Persei sub rupibus antri indignata sequi torquentem cornua Mithram.*' (Under the rocks of the Persian cave Mithras is forcing the horns [of the bull] unwilling to follow [him]).
27. Against Cumont, [5]1981, p. 34, and Turcan, 1981, p. 42.
28. Cf. Merkelbach, p. 124, and Turcan, 1981, pp. 51 and 98-99, who are discussing the iconographic representations of this scene and, correspondingly, the expressions 'Mithras Buklopos'/'Abactorem Bovum' in Firmicus Maternus, *De errore profanorum religionum* 5,1, and other texts.
29. Cf. Cumont, [5]1981, pp. 120-123; Lease, pp. 1311-1312; Lommel, pp. 211-212, and Vermaseren, 1963, pp. 67-70.
30. This fundamental criticism does effect nearly all other interpretations of the bull-slaying scene as well, such as Campbell, Hinnells (1975), Speidel, Vermaseren (1963) and Will.
31. Thus Campbell, pp. 15-21 and 25-28; Harsberg, pp. 25-26; Hinnells, 1975, pp. 290-303; Lincoln, pp. 506 ff.; Merkelbach, pp. 13, 198 and 202; Schwertheim, p. 41, and Turcan, 1981, pp. 41-42.
32. *Op.cit.*, pp. VII-VIII, 76-77, 86 ff., 199 ff. and 230 ff. In the same direction point the interpretations of Campbell, pp. 6-7, 18-19, 54 ff., 68 ff., 141 ff., 257 ff., 265 etc.; Gordon, 1972, pp. 97 ff.; Lincoln, pp. 506-507, and Speidel, pp. 41-47.
33. Cf. Merkelbach, pp. 77-133, 230 ff. and 244.
34. Thus also Bianchi (1975); Campbell, pp. 371 and 392, and Hinnells, 1971, p. 67.
35. Cf. Turcan 1975 (e.g. pp. IX-X, 26, 35 etc.) and 1981, pp. 67-69, 81 ff. and 110-112.

36. According to Campbell, such heavy transformations and reinterpretations really took place in the Mysteries of Mithras (pp. 261-262 and 392). Further, Campbell has tried to demonstrate that Mithraism in different geographical areas was ideologically rather heterogeneous (cf. pp. 4 and 392).
37. Cf. also Hinnells, 1975, pp. 303-304, and Lavagne, p. 271.
38. Cf. Campbell, pp. 181 ff. and 248-249; Cumont, ^{5}1981, pp. 1-10, 17, 20, 88-90 and 116-117; Merkelbach, pp. 1-72 (especially pp. 4-5, 15 and 23 f.); Schwertheim, pp. 9-13, and Turcan, 1981, pp. 5-11.
39. Cf. Lommel, pp. 207-211; Merkelbach, pp. 15, 24-25 and 201, and Schwertheim, pp. 41-46.
40. Cf. Vermaseren, 1956-1960, figs. 100, 226, 379, 454, 504 and 597. See also Turcan, 1981, p. 57.
41. Cf. Vermaseren, 1956-1960, figs. 87, 94, 193 and 194.
42. Cf. Vermaseren, 1956-1960, figs. 23, 323, 340 and 355.
43. Cf. Vermaseren, 1956-1960, II, p. 425.
44. Cf. note 25 and Campbell, pp. 71-72; Lommel, pp. 213-214; Merkelbach, pp. 16-17 and 201 ff.; Turcan, 1975, p. 74, and 1981, p. 53.
45. Cf. Vermaseren, 1956-1960, figs. 67, 84, 262, etc.
46. Cf. Vermaseren, 1956-1960, fig. 294, and Merkelbach, pp. 112, 115 and 131.
47. This is also the case in Iranian and other religions, cf. Lommel, pp. 214 ff., and Merkelbach, pp. 201 ff.
48. That the bull-slaying scene is to be interpreted as a sacrifice is maintained by the great majority of scholars, e.g. Cumont, ^{5}1981, pp. 120-123; Harsberg, pp. 25-26; Hinnells, 1975, pp. 305-312, and Turcan, 1981, pp. 104-109. Against this view, Will, pp. 528-531, argues primarily from a stylistical point of view. To his arguments may be added Vermaseren, 1956-1960, fig. 91, showing Mithras as the triumphant victor after having killed the bull-enemy.
49. Cf. Campbell, pp. 29-43, 54 ff. and 70 ff., especially pp. 35-36 and 41; Schwertheim, pp. 47-48, and Turcan, 1981, p. 40.
50. Cf. Vermaseren, 1956-1960, figs. 14, 46, 47, 49, 88, 91, 98, 102, 106, 114, 340-342 etc.
51. For this 'positive' interpretation of the accompanying animals, see also Campbell, pp. 15-21 and 25-28; Hinnells, 1975, pp. 292-300; Lincoln, pp. 506 ff., and Turcan, 1981, pp. 59 and 104 ff.
52. Cf. Vermaseren, 1956-1960, figs. 47, 48, 84, 88 etc. and 168.
53. Cf. Vermaseren, 1956-1960, figs. 93, 106, 114, 150, 195, 262, 274, 337, and 355.
54. Similarly, Harsberg, pp. 24-27; Hinnells, 1975, p. 309; Schwertheim, pp. 30-31; Turcan, 1975, pp. 82-83 and 85, and 1981, pp. 104-109 and especially p. 89: 'Dans le mythe mithraique, le salut alimentaire de la vie humaine et animale semble avoir eu plus d'importance qu'on ne croit'.
55. For descriptions of the mithraeum, see Campbell, pp. 6-10 and 44-90; Harsberg, pp. 29-33; Lavagne; Merkelbach, pp. 133 ff.; Schwertheim, pp. 51-57; Turcan, 1981, pp. 72-78, and Vermaseren, 1963, pp. 37-43.
56. Cf. Vermaseren, 1956-1960, figs. 25, 46, 48, 88, 106, 114, 123, 150, 154, 181 etc., and Turcan, 1981, pp. 72-73.

57. Cf. Vermaseren, 1956-1960, figs. 7, 13, 121, 130, 131 etc.
58. Cf. Vermaseren, 1956-1960, figs. 21, 180, 217, 275, 297, 323 etc., and Kane, pp. 344-348.
59. Cf. Vermaseren, 1963, p. 99.
60. Cf. Hinnells, 1975, pp. 304-305, and Turcan, 1981, p. 72, who emphasize that the bull-slaying scene and the scene of the mythological meal are interrelated. An opposing view is found in Kane's article where this author separates the mythological and the ritual meals.
61. Thus also Campbell, p. 323; Merkelbach, p. 134; Schwertheim, pp. 57-58, and, especially, Turcan, 1981, p. 72.
62. Cf. *Apologia* I, 66, quoted from Cumont, 1896, p. 20: 'ὅτι γὰρ ἄρτος καὶ ποτήριον ὕδατος τίθεται ἐν ταῖς τοῦ μυομένου τελεταῖς μετ' ἐπιλόγων τινων ...'.
63. Cf. *De praescriptione haereticorum* 40, quoted from Cumont, 1896, p. 51: 'Tingit et ipse quosdam ... (et si adhuc nemini, Mithra signat illic in frontibus milites suos,) celebrat et panis oblationem ...'.
64. Cf. note 17 above and Kane, p. 350; Merkelbach, p. 134, and Schwertheim, pp. 57-58 and 73. The finds of tableware mentioned by Merkelbach and Schwertheim point in the same direction.
65. According to Porphyrios (Eubulos), the Mithraic cave is an image of the world, cf. *De antro nympharum* 6, quoted from Cumont, 1896, p. 40: 'εἰκόνα φέροντος [αὐτῷ] τοῦ σπηλαίου τοῦ κόσμου, (ὃν ὁ Μιθρας ἐδημιούργησε) ...'. See also Campbell, pp. 49-50 and 95; Merkelbach, pp. 113 and 134; Schwertheim, p. 47; Turcan, 1975, p. 67, and 1981, p. 74.
66. Similarly Schwertheim, p. 46 and 58, and Turcan, 1981, pp. 65, 78, 93 and 104, but against Kane, pp. 343-351, who makes a sharp distinction between the mythical meal, its ritual reiteration in Roman Mithraism and the Mithraic cultic meal which according to Kane has nothing to do with the mythical meal nor is to be conceived of as a sacrament.
67. Thus also Schwertheim, pp. 58-61; Simon, p. 465, and Turcan, 1981, p. 78, whereas this view is rejected by Kane, cf. note 66.
68. The symbols of the Mithraic grades and the paintings found on the left wall in the mithraeum of Santa Prisca in Rome indicate the intimate interrelation between the gods and the humans, cf. Vermaseren-van Essen, p. 152: 'The gods have given the divine example, and it is now up to the μετέχοντες to follow this example in the divine service, for the salvation of their own souls'. Thus also Hinnells, 1975, p. 309.
69. Otherwise the idea of evil does not appear in the Mithraic sources.
70. Cf. especially Vermaseren, 1956-1960, fig. 91, and Gordon, 1972, pp. 96, 98 and 100; Harsberg, p. 19; Nock, pp. 111-113, and Turcan, 1981, p. 109, over against Simon, pp. 475-477.
71. Similarly, Gordon, 1972, pp. 95, 97 and 112; Harsberg, pp. 19-20; Turcan, 1975, pp. 130 and 133, and 1981, pp. 72-80 and 109-114.
72. Cf. especially Gordon, 1972, pp. 95 and 102 ff.; Harsberg, pp. 46-48; Turcan, 1981, pp. 31 ff. and 114, and Will, pp. 534-536.

BIBLIOGRAPHY:

Beskow, P., 'The Routes of the Early Mithraism', *Études Mithraiques, Acta Iranica* 17, Leiden 1978, 7-8.
Bianchi, U., 'Mithraism and Gnosticism', *Mithraic Studies*, 2, 1975, 457-465.
Bianchi, U., (ed.) *Mysteria Mithrae*, Leiden 1979.
Campbell, L.A., *Mithraic Iconography and Ideology*, Leiden 1968.
Cumont, F., *Textes et monuments figurés relatifs aux Mystères de Mithra*, I-II, Bruxelles 1896-1899.
Cumont, F., *Die Mysterien des Mithra*, Darmstadt [5]1981.
Gordon, R.L., 'Mithraism and Roman Society. Social Factors in the Explanation of Religious Change in the Roman Empire', *Religion*, 2, 1972, 92-121.
Gordon, R.L., 'Franz Cumont and the Doctrines of Mithraism', *Mithraic Studies*, 1, 1973, 215-248.
Gordon, R.L., (ed.) *Journal of Mithraic Studies*, 1-3, London 1976-1979.
Harsberg, E., *Mithras. Mysterier og monumenter i romerriget*, Copenhagen 1983.
Hinnells, J.R., 'Method and Message in Mithraism', *Religion*, 1, 1971, 66-71.
Hinnells, J.R., (ed.) *Mithraic Studies*, 1-2, Manchester 1975.
Hinnells, J.R., 'Reflexions on the Bull-Slaying Scene', *Mithraic Studies*, 2, 1975, 290-312.
Kane, J.P., 'The Mithraic Cult Meal in its Greek and Roman Environnement', *Mithraic Studies*, 2, 1975, 313-351.
Lavagne, H., 'Importance de la grotte dans le Mithriacisme en Occident', *Études Mithraiques, Acta Iranica* 17, Leiden 1978, 271-278.
Lease, G., 'Mithraism and Christianity: Borrowings and Transformations', *Aufstieg und Niedergang der römerischen Welt*, II, 23, 2, 1306-1332.
Lincoln, B., 'Mithra(s) as Sun and Saviour', *La soteriologia dei culti orientali nell' impero romano*, ed. U. Bianchi and M.J. Vermaseren, Leiden 1982, 505-526.
Lommel, H., 'Mithra und das Stieropfer', *Paideuma*, 3, 1949, 207-218.
Merkelbach, R., *Mithras*, Hain 1984.
Nilsson, M.P., *Geschichte der griechischen Religion*, I-II, München [2]1961, II, 667-679.
Nock, A.D., 'The Genius of Mithraism', *JRS*, 27, 1937, 109-113.
Schwertheim, E., 'Mithras, seine Denkmäler und sein Kult', *Antike Welt*, 10, 1979, 1-76.
Simon, M., 'Mithra, rival du Christ?', *Études Mithraiques, Acta Iranica* 17, Leiden 1978, 457-478.
Speidel, M.P., *Mithras-Orion, Greek Hero and Roman Army God*, Leiden 1980.
Turcan, R., *Mithras Platonicus. Recherches sur l'hellenisation philosophique du culte de Mithra*, Leiden 1975.
Turcan, R., *Mithra et le mithriacisme*, Paris 1981.
Vermaseren, M.J., (ed.) *Corpus Inscriptionum et Monumentorum Religionis Mithraicae*, I-II, Haag 1956-1960.
Vermaseren, M.J., *Mithras the Secret God*, London and New York 1963.
Vermaseren, M.J., (ed.) *Mithraica I-IV*, Leiden 1971-1982.

Vermaseren, M.J. and C.C. von Essen, *The Excavations in the Mithraeum of the Church of Santa Prisca in Rome*, Leiden 1965.
Wikander, S., 'Études sur les mystères de Mithras, I', *Vitenskaps-Societeten i Lund, Årsbok*, 1950, 5-46.
Will, E., 'Origine et nature du mithriacisme', *Études Mithraiques, Acta Iranica* 17 Leiden 1978, 527-536.

HERMETIC COMMUNITIES?

by Søren Giversen

Hermetic communities? Did such communities ever exist?

No remnants of Hermetic temples or ruins of buildings for religious purposes have been discovered till now. No traces of an organization of adherents have been found. No lists of officials from a Hermetic cult in charge of specific liturgical duties have come down to us, and neither do we know of any Hermetic hierarchies as we know them from all other religious bodies in the first to the third century A.D.

And to continue this line, there is no information available about the existence of a fixed canon of holy Hermetic scriptures as we know it from the Jews about the year 90 and a little later from the Christian church.

And we have no traces of manuals used to rule or regulate the life of the members of any Hermetic community, as we have the *Manual of discipline* from Qumran or the *Didache* from the first or second century, or the younger *Apostolic constitutions* or the *Didascalia* from the second to the fourth century.

In accordance with all these missing traces of Hermetic communities it is of course also a widespread belief among scholars that such a Hermetic community never existed — or scholars express themselves in very vague terms about the possibility of the existence of such a community.

In this short paper I do not intend to present so much material that this old view must be finally abandoned. Neither the limited time nor the special character of the source material will allow of any such decisive conclusion. What I wish to do here is to point out some important details, partly or completely overlooked, and at the same time to present a few observations made during my work on a translation into Danish of all the Hermetic tractates,[1] and later on also during the work with the translation of the rest of the Hermetic texts, the excerpts of Stobaeus, the citations and the newly discovered Hermetic tractate in the Armenian language and two new Hermetic writings in Coptic, which I hope, will be ready for publication this autumn.

Each of these details and observations may seem unimportant when looked upon in isolation, but taken as a whole it seems to me that in all essentials they point in the direction of a necessary review of the questions of Hermetic religious life and practice.

In an article Jean Pière Mahé[2] has rightly pointed to the fact that the Hermetic writings do not form a uniform corpus, especially with regard to an ascetic or encratitic way of life.

A similar view was taken by A.J. Festugière[3] in 1948. Festugière underlined that there is for instance an essential difference between two views of the world, both present in the *Corpus Hermeticum*. Its tractates may thus be divided into two groups:

1) the first group regards the world from a pantheistic-monistic view of the world as the work of God and consequently so filled with God that man should be able to recognize God in it. This is the view of tractates V, VIII and IX,
2) the second group has a dualistic view of the world, a world which is considered to be thoroughly bad. This opinion is found in tractates I, IV, VI, VII and XII.

In view of this great difference in world-view between the two groups of Hermetic writings, it seems even more desirable to make a deeper investigation of the Hermetic writings to discover possible remnants of a Hermetic community life — or perhaps the beginnings of such a life. Such an investigation could perhaps turn out to yield more nuances to our picture of the Hermetic writings.

The source material available for us today consists of texts only: the about twenty tractates, the excerpts from Stobaeus, the scattered fragments — about 40 — and the later discovered tractates in Armenian and Coptic. For practical reasons I shall on this occasion refer only to the tractates and not to the excerpts or fragments.

How does a community establish itself? How does it arise from a movement? And what kind of traces would such a process have left in our sources? — As criteria for the existence of a certain common, religious life of two or more participants we might take the exercise of one or more of the following items:

> preaching of conversion,
> the call for conversion,
> the reaction of the converts,
> further religious training,
> liturgical practise,
> sacramental rites as baptism and holy meal,
> the keeping of traditions,
> ethics.

Below, I shall try to illustrate some of these points with examples from the texts. It is, however, necessary to bear in mind that all the texts but perhaps two (Tr. VII and XVII) are philosophical, aiming at the discussion of various religious problems. In nearly all the texts, we therefore merely get the information wanted indirectly. Nearly all the tractates are thus doctrinal writings, of which only tractates X, XI, XII and XVI, *Asclepius*, *Kore Kosmu* and the Armenian *The definitions of Hermes* pretend to represent the total Hermetic teaching, whereas tractates II, IV, V, VI, VIII, IX, XIII and XIV intend to deal with special questions only.

In *Poimandres*, the narrator is called to preach (I,26): 'Why do you wait? Now that you have received everything, why not, then, be a guide for those who are worthy, in order that the human race be saved by God through you?'

This is a call to preach for other men. We also know how the newly converted preacher's sermon was. This is told in I,27, where he 'began to preach the beauty of piety and knowledge' for people: 'O nations, you earthborne men! You who have given yourself over to drunkenness, to sleep and to ignorance of God! Become sober and cease intoxicating yourselves, bewitched by unreasonable sleep.'

Tractate VII, in its entirety a sermon, has a very similar beginning: 'For how long will you endure, o men, intoxicated as you are, because you have drunk the unmixed word of ignorance, words which you are not able to keep but are already spitting out again? Be sober and cease ...'

This was a preaching of conversion. And we actually know how this sermon was received (I, 28): 'But when they had heard my teaching they followed me unanimously. But I say: 'Why, ye earthborne men, why have you surrendered to death although you are in possession of power sufficient to participate in immortality? Repent, ye who relied on an error. Repent, ye who have been in ignorance'.' Then it is said very realistically: 'Some of them, however, were mocking, and they went away, for they had surrendered to the camp of death. Other men, however, threw themselves at my feet and beseeched me to be instructed. And I lifted them up, and I became a guide for mankind, and I instructed them about the teaching, how and through what man is saved.'

When the newly converted people have received this basic teaching about salvation we hear about them again. I,29 says: 'But when it was the last part of the day, and the sunlight began to fade completely, I asked them to give praise to God, and when they had completed their praise to God each of them went home to his bed.'

Thus *Poimandres* has nearly the same information as is presented in the two last chapters of *Asclepius*. In chapter 40 Trismegistos says: 'I have now explained everything to you as far as it has been humanly possible, and as far as the divine being has wished it and permitted it. It remains now for us only to give thanks to God in prayer and then to take care of our body. For discussing the divine matters so much, it is as though we have satisfied our souls with food.'

In the following chapter, we are told how to say a prayer which, in my opinion, indicates that there existed certain customs or even rules for prayers, followed by Hermetists. The instruction in *Ascl.* 41 has the following wording: 'They began to pray to God with their eyes directed to the south, for when anyone wishes to pray to God at sunset he ought to look in that direction, just as he ought to look to the east at dawn'.

In the Hermetic Nag Hammadi text *The Eighth and the Ninth* in NH codex VI, the disciple is instructed about prayer. The disciple also has a vision, and he is instructed 'to sing a hymn to the father until the day when you take off the body'.

In *Asclepius* as well as in *Poimandres* and this Hermetic Nag Hammadi text we fortunately find the wording of such hymns.

In *Poimandres*, the narrator (I,31) initially brings a nine-fold praise of God. Each of its verses begins with the word 'hagios', and the entire hymn is divided into three stanzas of which the first is a call to him as God, the second is about his acting, the third about his being,

> Holy is God, the father of all things!
> Holy is God, whose will is completed through his own powers!
> Holy is God, who wisheth to be known, and is known by his own!

> Holy art thou, who created every being with thy word!
> Holy art thou, whom the entire nature depicteth!
> Holy art thou, whom the entire nature giveth not form!
>
> Holy art thou, who art stronger than every power!
> Holy art thou, who art greater than the greatest!
> Holy art thou, who art better than praises!

And then follows the prayer: 'Receive pure offerings in words from a soul and a heart which is directed unto thee, thou unspeakable, ineffable One, thou who wilt only be mentioned in silence'. The worshipper then asks never to lose his knowledge, hoping that he can enlighten his generation: 'my brethren, thy sons'. It concludes with a confession: 'Every man, who belongeth unto thee, wisheth together with thee to work for the sanctification' (I,31).

If we return to the *Asclepius* once more we find — here as well — a concluding praise of God in the form of a long prayer: 'We thank thou. Thou most high ...' and the long prayer ends with a prayer that their own knowledge may remain.

At this point I ought, perhaps, to mention the warnings in *Asclepius* as well as other Hermetic texts against offerings; the warnings are, however, not against offerings as such, but against offerings of anything but hymns.

In accordance with what I said at the outset I have here confined myself to liturgy and prayer. I could, however, also give examples which testify to *baptism*: a spiritual baptism and a wish to be baptized is found in *tractate IV*. *Asclepius* testifies to a *holy meal*: 'When we had thus prayed we went to a meal which was holy and without flesh'(41).

Two examples testify to the use of the word *temple*: In *Asclepius*, the long instruction takes place in *a sanctuary* (41), and *the Holy Book* which is to be written containing *The Eighth and the Ninth* is to be inscribed on steles and placed in the temple of Diospolis, according to the Coptic Hermetic text.[4] Here, for the first time we have, in a Hermetic text, connected with a fixed locality, a temple mentioned by name, either *Diospolis parva* or *Diospolis magna*.

In *The Eighth and the Ninth*, as well as in *Kore Kosmu*, the texts tell us about *holy books*.

In sum, we have examples of what could belong to a community life: prayer, hymns, liturgy, baptism, holy meal, temple and holy books.

NOTES:

1. Published as: *Den ukendte gud. Hermes-skrifterne i oversættelse ved Søren Giversen.* København: Gad 1983.
2. *Les textes de Nag Hammadi.* Colloque du Centre d'Histoire des Religions. Ed. par J.-E. Menard. (*Nag Hammadi Studies*; 7). Leiden 1975, 123-145.
3. *Kungl. Humanistiske Vetenskapssamfundet i Lund. Årsberättelse/Bulletin de la Societe Royale des Lettres de Lunda 1947-1948.* Lund 1948, p. 10.
4. NHC VI,61; cf. Martin Krause & Pahor Labib, *Gnostische und Hermetische Schriften aus Codex II und Codex VI* (Abh. d. Deutschen Archäologischen Instituts Kairo. Koptische Reihe; Band 2) Glückstadt 1971, p. 181.

ADAMAS AND THE FOUR ILLUMINATORS IN SETHIAN GNOSTICISM

by Jørgen Verner Hansen

One of the recurring themes in the Gnostic writings, which *Hans Martin Schenke* has classified as Sethian, is that of *Autogenes* and his four light- or illuminator-aions.[1] The names of these φωστῆρες are *Harmozel*, *Oroiael*, *Davithe*, and *Eleleth* (with frequent variations in the spelling). Primarily they function as the dwelling-places of respectively the heavenly Adam, called *Adamas*,[2] his son *Seth*, and the sons of Seth. With the aion of Eleleth there is some disagreement. While *The Gospel of the Egyptians* (NHC III,2 & IV,2) and *Zostrianos* (NHC VIII,1) hold this phoster-aion to be the place of the souls of the sons of Seth, *The Apocryphon of John* (NHC II,1; NHC III,1; NHC IV,1; BG 8502,2) maintains that those dwelling in Eleleth are the ones who did not repent at once, when gnosis was revealed to them, but persisted for a while in serving the evil archon.

In his short but very important paper *Das sethianische System nach Nag Hammadi-Handschriften*, in which Schenke introduced his theories on Sethian Gnosticism, these four aions are interpreted as symbolizing the four world-periods of Adam, Seth, 'die Ursethianer', and the historical Sethians, and also as constituting a sort of paradises for these four categories of the pneumatic part of mankind.[3] This interpretation was taken up by *Carsten Colpe* who tried to supply it with the necassary Iranian and Mesopotamian background-material, which Schenke also had in mind as the ultimate source for this Sethian conception.[4]

From quite another angle of Gnostic studies a new interpretation has recently seen the light. *Simone Petrement*, prominent among scholars who believe that Gnosticism is best explained as being merely a bi-produkt of Christianity, attempts in her paper entitled *Les quatre illuminateurs, sur le sens et l'origine d'un thème gnostique* to explain this very complex

Sethian theme by deriving it primarily from Valentinian speculations on the figure of Jesus Christ.[5]

Hitherto, this theme has generally been taken as an indication that the inner structure of the systems in which it appears — whether one calls them Sethian or something else — is essentially of a non-Christian — if not pre-Christian provenance. Nobody has attached any importance to the fact that *Ap.John* and *Gos.Eg.* place Christ in the Harmozel-aion together with Adamas, and that the latter even has Jesus in Oroiael together with Seth. This was seen to be just another sign that the Sethian systems had been christianized in a rather superficial way simply by putting in Christ and Jesus where there happened to be room.

It is this generally accepted picture of the relations between non-Christian and Christian Gnosis which Simone Petrement now tries to turn upside down by making Valentinian Gnosis the source of the theme of the four illuminators, and consequently — considering the prime importance of this theme — the Sethian Gnostiscism as a whole is also, according to Petrement, to be regarded as a post-Valentinian creation, with the Christian-Gnostic text (I would say christianized Gnostic text) *The Apocryphon of John* as maybe the earliest example of this Valentinian-derived Sethian or, according to *Irenaios*, Barbelognostic heresy.

Although I find Petrement's theory an interesting new way of seeing things, I think that there are so many things that speak against her that she can't possibly be right. However, it is not my intention to deliver a detailed critique of her position. Instead I want to present another interpretation of the theme in question; one which also runs counter to the one advocated by Schenke and Colpe, and which is concerned only with the meaning and function of the theme within its Sethian context. The delicate question of origin I prefer to leave untouched.

In a dissertation on Sethian Gnosticism, written in 1981 before the publication of Petrement's paper, and also before the appearance on print of the papers delivered at the Yale seminar on Sethian Gnosticism, I attempted to extract the meaning of the concept of the four illuminators by connecting it with the speculations on the Son-figure of the Sethian triad.[6] And it is the results then achieved which I would now like to summerize and — to a certain extent — to develop a little further.

In Sethian theology Adamas is a very important figure. In *The Three Steles of Seth* (NHC VII,5) the Sethian triad is invoked in three hymns. The first one is addressed to the triadic Son, Adamas, the Father of Seth. The second to the Mother, *Barbelo*, or *Protophanes*, and the third to the

Father, *Kalyptos*, the hidden God. This pleromatic structure is very simple; there are no additional speculations on hypostases like *Nous*, *Logos*, *Ennoia* etc., such as we find in other Sethian writings. There are just three persons, with Seth functioning as the archetypal Gnostic invoking them as the fourth.

But in this apparent simplicity we must not overlook the fact that Adamas is described as the thrice-male, divided into a pentad and given to the seed of Seth in triple power, and that one of the epithets given to Adamas is *Autogenes* (119,16). These informations make it possible to relate this Son-figure to the more elaborate speculations on the Son in other Sethian texts, first of all in *Ap.John*.

Common to the four versions of this text is that the epithet *Autogenes* is attached to Christ, and also attached to Christ is the *pleroma* of the four *phosteres* (II 8,20-26; III 12,16-24; IV 13,4-?; BG 34,8-15). In the BG version (51,2-20) we are told that the Father at the request of *Sophia* sends out Autogenes and the four lights in the type of the angels of the first archon to advise *Jaldabaoth* to blow into the face of Adam something of his spirit, i.e. the spirit which he has taken over or stolen from Sophia. In the parallel passage in the long version of NHC II we find some interesting variations. First, it is not the Father but the *Metropator*, the Mother-Father, who is requested by Sophia, the Mother as she is called, and second, the legation is said to consist of five *phosteres* (the Greek word is used, whereas the BG version has the Coptic ⲟⲩⲟⲉⲓⲛ which simply means light) (II 19,15-27). From this we can conclude that Autogenes — whom all the versions in this special context fail to identify as Christ — is conceived as being a *phoster* too.

The *pleroma* of the triadic Son is thus composed of five *phosteres*: Autogenes and his four illuminators. Together they constitute a divine quintet — or maybe better — a quinity or a pentad, because it is this differentation of the Son which I think that the *Steles Seth* alludes to when it describes *Adamas Autogenes* as divided into a pentad.[7]

In *Ap.John* Autogenes and Adamas apear as two different entities, but according to Schenke, their original oneness is reflected in the fact that both are associated with the Harmozel-aion.[8] The relation between Adamas and Autogenes presents an interesting problem. In other Sethian writings Adamas is described as the eye of Autogenes. Thus we read in *Zost.* that 'Adamas is the [perfect] man, because he is the eye of Autogenes, an ascending knowledge of his, because the Autogenes-God is a word of the perfect *Nous* of truth' (30,4-9). Later in the same text (127,

15-128,6) it is said that the Autogenes-God stands within an *aion*, and that the Autogenes-aions of the four *phosteres* are within him. This is in good accordance with the notion of the four illuminators as residences of Adamas, Seth, and the seed of Seth. In the same way as Adamas as the eye is a part of Autogenes, thus Seth and the holy seed dwelling in the other aions are also conceived as being parts of the Autogenes-aion. Together they constitute, so to say, the elements of his spiritual body.

Another way to express this notion is to say that the Autogenes-God is made up of four aions contained in one aion, and this is exactly the way *Zost.* explains the relation between these five aions. 'The Autogenes-God is the first *archon* of his aions and of the messengers (ἄγγελος) as his parts; for those who are four in him individually create the fifth aion at one time. The fifth aion exists in one. It is the four who [are] the fifth, part by part' (19,6-15). In this way Autogenes *is* the four aions, i.e. the four illuminators. The structure is 4 – 1 – 5. The four elements united make the *quinta essentia*, Autogenes.

Another entity, which must be regarded as identical with Autogenes or Adamas or both, is the *thrice-male child*, a prominent figure in *Zost.*, and particularly in *Gos.Eg.*. In *Zost.* we find a passage which indicates that Adamas and Autogenes are conceived as being at the same time a unity and two separate entities, and furthermore, both identical with the thrice-male child (13,1-7). First the triad is mentioned. It consist of the unborn *Kalyptos*, the great *Protophanes*, i.e. Barbelo, and as the Son we find the *perfect child* with his eye Adamas. From this we can deduce that the child is Autogenes, but in the following lines, where *Zostrianos* calls upon the child of the child *Ephesech*, it becomes evident that Adamas is also the child, because when the child of the child appears, it presents itself as the son of the Father, the perfect man. This proves that Ephesech, as Schenke indicated in his 1974-paper, is identical with Seth, and that his Father, Adamas, is the child, the perfect thrice-male child.[9]

The relation between Autogenes, Adamas, and the child in *Zost.* proves their essential identity; an identity which also seems to be implied in *Gos.Eg.*. The phosterological scheme in this text is very clearly expounded – with enumerations of *syzygies* and *deacons* (III 51,14-53,12; IV 63,8-65,5) – but unfortunately, this clarity is absent when it comes to speculations on the Son-figure to which the illuminator-pleroma – as in other texts - is closely connected.

The rather badly damaged p. 60 of Codex IV relates the forthcoming of the great *Logos Autogenes* who with his word establishes the four aions.¹⁰ Logos then brings praise to the great invisible Spirit, 'the place where the man rests'. This results in the forthcoming of *Mirothea*, 'the Mother of the holy incorruptibles ones'. She gives birth to Adamas, 'the first man, the eye of the light'. Adamas and Logos Autogenes then mingle with each other, whereby a 'logos of man' comes into being. In spite of this mingling together, the text continues to speak about them in the plural. Thus the relation between them appears to be exactly the same as in *Zost.*. The subtle balance between unity and duality is also reflected in the passage relating the birth of Seth and the four illuminators (III 50,17-51,22; IV 62,16-63,17). Together Adamas and Autogenes bring praise to the whole pleroma and ask for a power and eternal strenght for Autogenes for the completion of the four aions, and for Adamas they ask for a son. This request results in the appearance of *Prophaneia* who gives birth to the four illuminators and Seth. Prophaneia is an interesting figure. As the mother of Seth she must in some way or another have been modelled over the figure of Eve. If she is conceived as a sort of female creative aspect of the androgynous Adamas, then she is an appropriate mother of the four illuminators which function as residences for the four categories of the differentiated Autogenes. In other words, she is then the creatrice of the spacial dimension in which the ideal unfolding of Adamas Autogenes takes place, that is, his differentiation into a holy seed destined to be incarnated on earth; a holy seed stretching from Adam via Seth to the Sethian Gnostics responsible for the writing.

The puzzling thing in *Gos.Eg.* is, however, that neither Adamas nor Autogenes are clearly described as being the Son in the triadic scheme. But a closer examination of the triadic speculations — seen in the light of the information we already have gathered from other texts — may reveal that both Autogenes and Adamas are in fact to be regarded at least as aspects of the Son-figure.

In *Gos.Eg.* the triad, Father, Mother, and Son, originates through a self-unfolding of the supreme invisible Spirit, not through emanations as e.g. in *Ap.John*. The triad, it is said, the Father brought forth from his bosom (III 41,23f.; IV 51,15f.). From the same place *Domedon Doxomedon*, the aion of the aions, came forth (III 41,13f.; IV 51,2f.). This aion too represents the self-unfolding of the supreme Father: 'The Father of the great light [who came] forth from the silence, he is the [great] *Doxomedon-aion*, in which the [thrice-male] child rests', it is stated (III 43,13-17; IV 53,9-15).

The Doxomedon-aion is — as *Alexander Böhlig* and *Frederik Wisse* have shown — a collective and spacial entity, who encompasses the heavenly realm.[11] He is the aion needed by the Father to manifest himself as a kind of second god, a differentiated god. But the Father is not only differentiated into a triad, but into a double triad. In the narrative this is already anticipated in the description of the forthcoming of the Doxomedon-aion, because here the text surprises us by stating that the Son came forth as the fourth, the Mother as the fifth, and the Father as the sixth (III 41,15-19; IV 51,2-11). The meaning of this only becomes clear when some pages later the appearance of a second triad is described. This triad, which we must imagine as being a reflection of the first triad, consists of the aforementioned thrice-male child, the male virgin *Iouel*, and the child of the child *Esephech* (III 44,9-?; IV 54,13-56,22).

The Doxomedon-aion is filled with many other spiritual powers and glories and incorruptions, and a throne is established in it — maybe the throne of the thrice-male child, but the basic structure of this pleroma consists of these two triads:

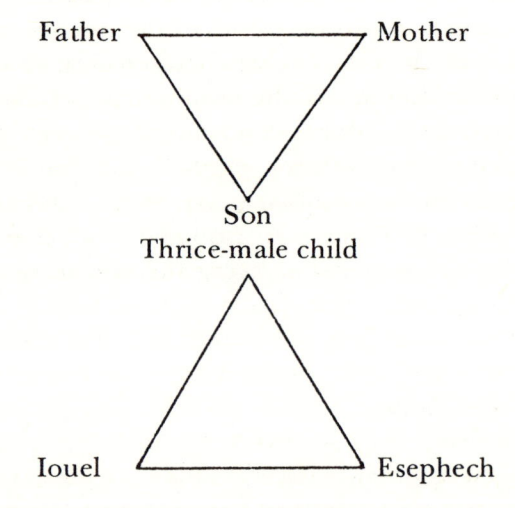

```
Father              Mother
     \             /
      \           /
       \         /
        \       /
         \     /
          \   /
           Son
    Thrice-male child
          / \
         /   \
        /     \
       /       \
      /         \
     /           \
    /             \
 Iouel           Esephech
```

From *Zost.* we know that Esephech/Ephesech can be identified as Seth, and the thrice-male child as Adamas Autogenes. In the pleromatic system of *Gos.Eg.* as schematized above, the child corresponds to the Son, and actually, in some of the enumerations of these beings in connection with presentations of praise, the Son is not mentioned. In his place we find instead the thrice-male child (f.ex. III 49,22f.; IV 61,23f.). If these two representations of the Son have become fused, then the Doxomedon-aion is reduced to five persons, a quinity or a pentad with the thrice-male Son in the center. This Son is Adamas, and his son is the child of the child Esephech/Seth. If we consider the second triad to be a reflection of the first one, then the thrice-male child reflects the Father, Iouel the Mother, and Esephech the Son. However, it is not that simple, because when the second triad appeared, the Son — it was said — came fourth, i.e. as the thrice-male child, the Mother fifth, i.e. as Iouel, and the Father sixth, i.e. as Esephech. It may seem strange that the Father is equated with Esephech/Seth, but this is not more strange than the fact that the trice-male child is called *Telmael Telmael Heli Heli Machar Machar Seth*, a name which implies that he too is some form of Seth (III 62,2; IV 73,12.

The Doxomedon-aion represents the first stage in the development and differentiation of the one supreme God, and the relation between the different entities is still characterized by a great deal of contamination. In this sense it is a true pleroma. Father, Son, and Grandson are still just three aspects of the male half of the divinity, and likewise the Mother Barbelo and Iouel, both characterized as male virgins, represent two interchangeable aspects of the predominantly female half (sexual differentiation is of course not very advanced either).[12]

If the Doxomedon-aion is thus composed of a double Father-Mother-Son triad, connected in a way that make them a quinity of three male and two female aspects of the one unfolded God, then the words concluding the description of the Doxomedon-aion make sense: 'And [thus] he was completed, namely the [Father], the Mother, the [Son], the five seals, the unconquerable power which is the great [Christ] of all the incorruptible ones' (IV 56,23-57,1). However, one thing that doesn't make sense at first sight is that the quinity, i.e. the five seals, seems to be identified with Christ, but actually this is in perfect accordance with the likewise strange assertion that Logos Autogenes is the son of Christ (IV 60,1-8). If Christ has been integrated into the system by being identified with the Doxomedon-aion, then it is the son of this aion, or rather in this aion, who — when emanated — appears as Logos Autogenes. His subsequent mingling with Adamas can no longer surprise us, because Adamas is none other than the thrice-male child, the Son in the Doxomedon-aion.

The logic in this subtle mythological play with names and concepts designating the Son is further emphazised by the fact that the child is called the thrice-male child of the great Christ (III 44,22; IV 55,11). Christ is the five-fold Doxomedon-aion in which the thrice-male Son rests. When he comes forth as Logos Autogenes Adamas, a new stage in the divine differentiation has begun.

In *Ap.John* we find the same basic structure, but the names and concepts are somewhat different from those in *Gos.Eg.*. In the long versions in Codex II and IV, the first aion, the *eikon*, which the Father emanates, is described among other things as Barbelo, the *Metropator*, the first man, the thrice-male, the thrice-powerful, the thrice-named androgynous one, the first to come forth, i.e. *Protophanes* (II 5,4-11; IV 7,20-27), but also as the *pentas-aion* of the Father, the androgynous pentas-aion which is the *decas-aion* which is the Father (II 6,8-10; IV 9,8-11). Thus the Barbelo-aion can be compared to the Doxomedon-aion of *Gos.Eg.* in that it represents the self-unfolding of the supreme Father, structured as a pentad. The Barbelo-aion is a second God, a creative Metropator-God, and the Son, Christ, the divine Autogenes, whom the Father-Mother-God begets, is then the third God or the third stage in the differentiation of God. This is the meaning — I think — of the very condensed words found in Codex III: 'He completed himself, the great invisible Spirit, the divine Autogenes, the Son of Barbelo, in an unfolding of the great invisible Spirit' (11,3-6). It is the word $\pi\alpha\rho\acute{\alpha}\sigma\tau\alpha\sigma\iota\varsigma$ which I — following *Martin Krause* — translate as 'unfolding' (Entfaltung). The same word is used in connection with the four illuminators who are described as a 'parastasis of Autogenes' (11,17-19).[13]

In *Ap.John* the Barbelo-aion is termed the first man. That means that the invisible Spirit has transformed himself into an androgynous man. The Son of this man is Autogenes. He is the $\upsilon\iota\grave{o}\varsigma\ \tau o\tilde{\upsilon}\ \alpha\nu\vartheta\rho\acute{\omega}\pi o\upsilon$, and therefore he can easily be identified with Christ, as all the four versions in fact do.

However, that Christ is neither the original *Son of Man* nor the original Autogenes can be deduced from the description of the birth of Seth in his terrestial form. In Codex II we read that Adam knew the likeness of his own *Prognosis* (= Eve), and brought forth the likeness of the Son of Man (24,34-25,2). The notion that Seth is the image of the Son of Man is — as *Birger A. Pearson* has demonstrated — derived from *Gen.* 5,3 wherein Seth is born as a son in his own, that is, in Adam's likeness.[14] In relation to *Ap.John* this implies that the Son of Man, in whose likeness Seth is born, is the heavenly Adam, i.e. Adamas.

Being the Son of Man, this Adamas is not only the one placed in the

Harmozel-aion together with Christ Autogenes, but also and originally the Son of the first man, Metropator, the Barbelo-aion. Here we can be fairly sure that a piece of the unchristianized Sethian myth shines through, and this — I think — is also the case with the words spoken to Sophia (to the Demiurge in other texts) by a voice from heaven: 'The Man exists and the Son of Man', says the voice. These words refer to Metropator as the first man, and Adamas as the Son of Man, and — as it is said very clearly — it is in the likeness of Metropator that the archons model their man from clay (II 14,13ff.). That gives us the following structure:

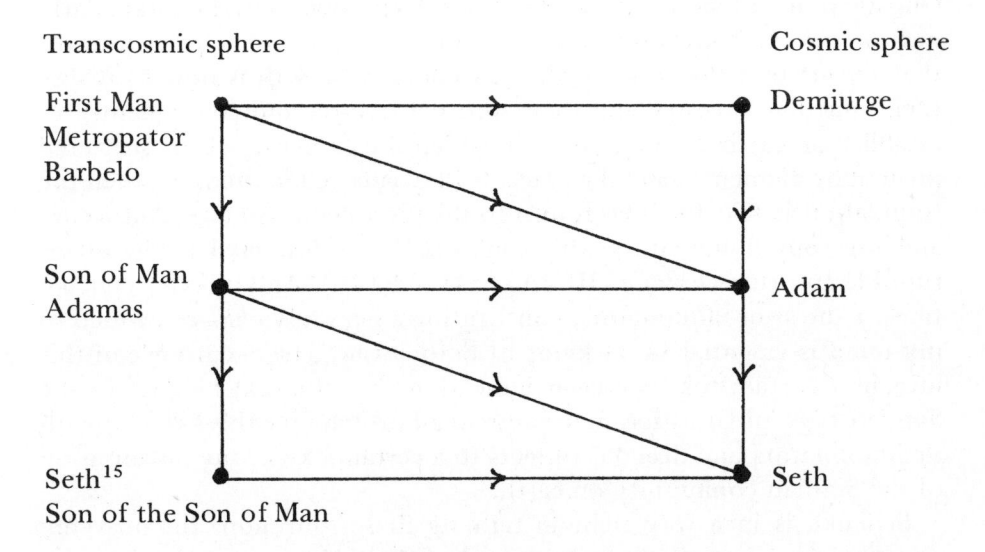

Transcosmic sphere   Cosmic sphere

First Man   Demiurge
Metropator
Barbelo

Son of Man   Adam
Adamas

Seth[15]   Seth
Son of the Son of Man

      Vertical lines mark the direct 'genealogical' relationship
      Horizontal lines mark the counterpart-relationship
      Oblique lines mark the 'iconical' relationship

In *Gos.Eg.* an unspecified God reveals himself to *Sakla*, the Demiurge, telling him that Man exists and the Son of Man, and — as in *Ap.John* — it is in the likeness (εἰκων) of this God that Adam is formed (III 59,1-9). Although the Doxomedon-aion of *Gos.Eg.* is not described as having the form of a man, there can hardly be any doubt that this second God is also conceived as the first Man. Just like the Barbelo-aion in *Ap.John*, the Doxomedon-aion represents the Gnostic concept of a *Mundus Intelligibilis*; an aion pregnant with the archetypes of everything spiritual:

powers, glories, incorruptions, and thrice-male races, but first of all with the Son of Man. When the archetypal content is born or emanated from this aion, it takes the form of the pleroma of Adamas Autogenes, the dwelling-place of the whole spiritual generation, the seed of Seth. With this the process of differentiation has come to an end and the pleroma is now ready to be incarnated on earth as the pneumatic elements inspired into the Adam-body and inherited by Seth and his descendants.

With the seed of Seth dispersed on earth the differentiation or multiplication of the divine principle has reached its maximum, and — from a Gnostic point of view — its lowest point deep down into the sarkic darkness of the Archons. From there the only way forward runs backwards; that means that the task for the descendants of Seth is now to realise their spiritual ancestry and their spiritual nature, and consequently to establish on earth a congregation in which the gathering of the scattered pneumatic elements can take place. If they succeed in doing so, then the foundation is laid for their return to the pleroma of Adamas Autogenes and the four illuminators which in *Gos.Eg.* is described as the incorruptible spiritual *ekklesia* (III 55,2f.; IV 64,14f.). And it is this conception of the four illuminators, constituting a heavenly *ekklesia*, which to my mind is essential to all kinds of Sethianism. The occurrence of this idea in a certain text is a clear indication that the text belongs to the Sethian type of Gnosticism, because in all probability this *ekklesia* with its illuminators and deacons reflects to a certain extent the organisation of the Sethian community on earth.

Schenke is in a way right in terming these four aions the heavenly paradises of Adam, Seth, and the seed of Seth. However, a very important aspect escapes his attention, namely the relation of the four aions to Adamas Autogenes; a relation which in *Zost.* is expressed in the way that the four aions together constitute the one Autogenes-aion which is the fifth. Considering that Adamas and Autogenes are in fact inseparable entities, the four illuminator-aions can be interpreted as representing in ideal form the scattering or multiplication of the *protoplast* Adam, his division into Seth and his holy seed, or the Adamases as they are called in another Sethian text, *The Thought of Norea* (NHC XI,2-29,1).[16]

Speculations on the scattering and rejoining af Adam/Adamas appear to have been a main concern for the Sethian Gnostics, and quite naturally, since the reintegration of Adamas means the salvation of the Sethians.

The Sethian tractate, *The Trimorphic Protennoia* (NHC XIII,1), describes the Son of God, the Christ, the God who came into being by himself, as standing in his own light that surrounds him who is the eye of the light (38,3-6). Although the names Adamas and Autogenes do not occur in the text, this is, nevertheless, a clear allusion to the concept of the light Autogenes with Adam functioning as his eye. Likewise, I think that it is into this light of Autogenes that the 'Sons of Man', the holy seed of the Son of Man, shall be placed at the end of time. In the words terminating the tractate, Protennoia — revealing herself as the Son of Man — says, 'I am unrestrained together with my seed, and my seed, which is mine, I shall [place] into the holy light' (50,17-19). This light is also called the light-place of his, i.e. the Gnostic's Fatherhood (48,30), and this Fatherhood refers not to the supreme Father, but to Adamas, because in the same context dealing with the salvation of the holy seed, the gathering together of the Sons of Man implies that 'the thought of the creature which [is scattered] will present a single appearance' (49,36-37). In other words, the spiritual element in Adam, his thought, which is scattered into the holy seed of Seth, will eventually become united into a single appearance, i.e. Adamas, the Son of Man.

In *Zost.* the Gnosis connected with what appears to be the most spiritual degree of baptism also deals with the mystery of dividing and joining. Ephesech says to Zostrianos, 'By knowing the origin of these, how they all appear in a single head and how they all are joined and divided, and how those who have been divided join again, and how the parts [join] with the wholes and the species and [races] — if one knows these things, he has washed in the washing of the Hidden One (Kalyptos)' (23,7-17). In the dialogue with Ephesech, Zostrianos later returns to this mystery asking Ephesech to tell him of 'the scattering of the man who is saved, and who those are who mixed with him, and who those are who are divided from him in order that the living elect might know' (45,4-9). Unfortunately, in the answer to this question Ephesech does not speak of the scattering of the man, but concentrates only on the salvation of the selfbegotten ones, the *autogeneis*, the seed of Seth belonging to the Autogenes-aion which —as we know — encompasses the four selfbegotten aions, the four phosteres.

However, in a previous description of these four phosteres we find what I believe is another reference to the mystery of dividing and joining. Harmozel, the illuminator of the first aion in which Adamas is dwelling, is described as 'a divison of the God of [....] and a joining of soul' (29,2-4). The Coptic word used for 'joining' is ϨΟΤΠ and this word often translates the Greek verb, ἁρμόζειν, which has the stem, ἁρμογ-. In my dissertation I proposed that the name Harmozel is composed of *harmoz-* to which is added the Hebrew *el* which in Gnosticism is frequently used as a sort of divinising suffix to Greek words or names, e.g. *Poimael* in *Gos.Eg.*. Support for this etymology is also found in *Irenaios'* description of the Barbelo-gnostics. The first illuminator is there called *Armoges*, a name clearly derived from the stem ἁρμογ- (*Adv.Haer.* I 29,2). Harmozel/Armoges is then the one who joins.

To me this etymology applies very well to the general conception of the four illuminators as a spiritual *ekklesia* in which the scattering of Adam is prefigured, and in which the joining of the dispersed elements, the Adamases, also takes place.

The concept of dividing and joining associated with Harmozel probably also sheds some light on the words spoken by Adamas in *Ap.John* immediately after his instalment into the Harmozel-aion. Adamas blesses the great invisible Spirit and says. 'All things have come into existence through you and the All will surely return to you' (II 9,7-8). Harmozel is apparently a guarantee for such a happy ending of the divine drama, and maybe this explains why the Barbelo-gnostics of Irenaios call Armoges the Saviour.

When I read Petrement's paper on the four illuminators, I was surprised to find that she proposes the same etymology to the name Harmozel, but I must admit that I was less surprised to find that she connects it — not with Adamas — but with Jesus Christ, and especially with the Valentinian conception of Jesus. According to the Ptolemaic system described by Irenaios, all the aions of the pleroma contribute to the creation of Jesus by giving and uniting harmoniously their most beautiful and bright elements (*Adv.Haer.* I 2,6). In this description it is the word harmoniously (ἁρμόδιως) which has led Petrement to suppose that the illuminator-aion, in which Adamas and Christ are placed, has its name from this harmonization of the pleromatic elements into the star of the pleroma, as Jesus is called.[17]

Here I don't want to dicuss the arguments which Petrement advances in support of her theory, but just mention that also the names of the other three illuminators she manages to bring into connection with speculations on Christ or Jesus. Why the names Oroiael, Davithe, and Eleleth were chosen by the Sethians to designate the dwelling-places of Seth, the sons of Seth, and those slow to repent, or the souls of the sons of Seth, is still a mystery to me and I am not able to add anything to the not very convincing proposals which already have been advanced. Only I want to mention that the problem concerning the identity of the original inhabitants of the aion of Eleleth can probably be solved through a piece of Sethian mythology found in *The Apocalypse of Adam* (NHC V,5), provided that this text represents Sethianism in one of its oldest known forms, which I believe it does.[18] In the mythology of *Apoc.Adam* the generation descending from Noah and his sons *Sem*, *Cham* and *Japheth* will serve the evil archon *Sakla*, and therefore they will be the natural adversaries of the spiritual generation of Seth. However, 400 000 of the seed of Cham and Japheth will desert from the slavery in which Sakla holds them, and — the text says — 'they will enter into another land and sojourn with those men who came forth from the great eternal knowledge', that is, the seed of Seth (73,12-20).

In the extant Sethian literature this is the only instance in which we hear of a large number of people changing their minds and joining the Sethian community. According to descent they are not Sethians and therefore have to be distinguished from the pure Sethians descending from Adam and Seth, but, nevertheless, they are accepted as members of the Sethian *ekklesia*, and this, I think, is only possible because their archetypes are already present in the aion of Eleleth. The 400 000 represent those who are slow to repent.

By this myth and the idea that those who continue to serve the archon, but eventually repent, belong to Eleleth, the Sethians offer an explanation to the otherwise disturbing fact that people obviously having a pagan or otherwise non-Sethian background join the community of the pure Sethians. In Sethian ekklesiology Eleleth is, so to say, the aion of the Sethian proselyts.

Probably because Sethianism in the course of time developed in a direction away from its Jewish roots and towards the current philosophy of the time, this myth of the 400 000 from the seed of Cham and Japheth has been abandoned, and the aion of Eleleth transformed into the dwelling-place of the souls of the sons of Seth, the sons themselves still dwelling in Davithe. This separation of the souls from the sons of Seth maybe has a certain philosophical flavour (a distinction between nous/pneuma and psyche), but appears to be carried out rather arbitrarily, and there is nothing in the otherwise very variated Sethian mythology to justify it. At least these souls do not represent the chosen ones from a certain world-period as should be the case according to Schenke's theory.

In order to obtain a basis for my theory concerning the four illuminators as constituting the spiritual 'body' of the Son of Man, Adamas Autogenes, I have dealt at some length with the five-fold structure of the pleroma of the first Man and of the Son of Man, and to conclude this paper I now want to carry this theory a little further by relating it to the few and scattered informations we have on the cult practised in the Sethian community.[19]

To judge from *Gos.Eg.* the term 'the five seals' designates the Doxomedon-aion as a quinity, but it is also applied as a cultic term. In this sense the five seals have to do with a baptism which also involves instructions about the receivers, the paralemptores, who are commissioned to receive the saved Sethians in the spiritual *ekklesia* (III 65,26-66,8; IV 78,1-10). These receivers are the deacons of the four illuminators; *Gamaliel*, *Gabriel*, *Samblo*, and *Abrasax* are their names. In *Trim.Prot.* they are given a more active function, namely that of schnatching away the Sethian Gnostic from the world and bringing him up to the light-place of his Fatherhood, in which he receives the five seals from the light of Protennoia, and is granted to partake in the mystery of Gnosis (48,26-35). As already mentioned, this light-place, I believe, refers to the pleroma of Adamas, the spirituel *ekklesia*. The important thing, however, is that this snatching away is the last of five different rites performed for the salvation of the Sethian Gnostic. In the first ritual the Gnostic is dressed in a robe of light. This appears to be a sort of baptismal robe, because the next ritual is the baptism in the water of life. Thereupon follows an intronization, and as the fourth ritual — before being snatched away — the Gnostic is glorified with the glory of the Fatherhood (48,15-35). When the five seals later on (49,26-32) are described as something the Gnostic is in possession of already in this life, we must conclude that these five rituals, culminating in the conveyance of the five seals by Protennoia, represent a cult which has been practised in the Sethian community, maybe as a salvific initiation which guarantees an escatological salvation to the individual.

Compared to *Gos.Eg.* there is, however, a clear difference. In *Gos.Eg.* the five seals appear to relate solely to baptism and instruction about the receivers. In *Trim.Prot.* baptism seems to be only an initial stage in the cult of salvation. The one thing in common is the role played by the deacons of the four illuminators. They arrange the restoration of the Sethians into the pleroma of Adamas Autogenes, the spiritual *ekklesia*.

In *Zost.* an embarrassing amount of seals and baptisms are described, but they are all transferred to the transmundane spheres. However, one thing I find is of some significance, and that is the fact that Zostrianos is baptized five times during his journey through the pleroma of Autogenes. The first four baptisms, which follow in a row, are explicitly associated with the illuminator-aions. The first baptism in Eleleth also involves another purifying ritual and a revelation in which Zostrianos is written in glory, and lastly follows a sealing. Thereby Zostrianos becomes a root-seeing messenger which means — I think — that he is now able to see and comprehend the roots of the generation of Seth, the place from which they were dispersed. The second baptism makes Zostrianos a messenger of the perfect male race, and by the third baptism he becomes a holy messenger, and the fourth baptism makes him a perfect messenger (6,7-7,22). The message he is now able to convey concerns, of course, the holy seed of Seth, as it is stated in the end when Zostrianos has returned to earth and started preaching the truth to the world (130,1ff.). The 4 - 1 - 5 structure of the Autogenes-aion apparently also applies to the baptisms in this aion, because only 46 pages later we hear about the fifth baptism in the name of Autogenes, and by this baptism Zostrianos becomes divine (53,15-25).

Although the succeeding baptisms in the aions of the Mother Protophanes and the Father Kalyptos are considered to be more elevated, these five baptisms in Autogenes are certainly of prime importance and seem to be especially connected with the salvation of the Sethians. Nowhere in the text the five seals are mentioned, neither is the Doxomedon-aion, but considering that the five entities in this aion are prominently represented in the text, and that the pleroma of Autogenes is structured as a quinity, it is not too far-fetched, I think, to suggest that the five baptisms may reflect the rites of the five seals as they were carried out in at least one Sethian community, a community deeply involved in the mystical philosophy of late antiquity.[20]

Just as the Gnosis of the Sethians could be expressed mythologically in a variety of ways without loosing its inner core, so it seems that the rites termed the five seals could also take different forms in the different Sethian communities without losing the essential meaning, the salvific potency of bringing the Sethians back to their roots in the aion of the selfbegotten Adamas. The five seals serve the reintegration of the scattered Adam, but ultimately the aim is the 'indifferentiation' of God, the transformation of divinity from the painful state of multiplicity into its original blissful oneness.

NOTES:

1. Hans Martin Schenke, 'The Phenomenon and Significance of Gnostic Sethianism' in *The Rediscovery of Gnosticism*, Proceedings of the International Conference on Gnosticism at Yale, March 1978, vol. II, 'Sethian Gnosticism', ed. Bentley Leyton, *Studies in the History of Religions* (Supplement to Numen) XLI, Leiden 1981, 588-616.
   The theme occurs explicitly in *The Apocryphon of John* (NHC II,1; NHC III,1; NHC IV,1; BG 8502,1); *The Gospel of the Egyptians* (NHC III,2; NHC IV,2); *Zostrianos* (NHC VIII,1); *Melchizedek* (NHC IX,1); *Trimorphic Protennoia* (NHC XIII,1); *The Untitled Text in the Bruce Codex*, and implicitly in *The Hypostasis of the Archons* (NHC II,4); *The Apocalypse of Adam* (NHC V,5); *The Thought of Norea* (NHC IX,2).
   The Absence of the theme in *The Three Steles of Seth* (NHC VII,5) and *Allogenes* (NHC XI,3) is due to the fact that these Sethian texts are only dealing with the spiritual world beyond the sphere of the four illuminators.
2. In some of the texts we find the name ΠΙΓΕΡΑΔΑΜΑC (*Ap.John* NHC II,1; *Steles Seth*; *Zost.*; *Melch.*). Agreement on meaning and etymology has not been reached; see the latest attempt at solving the problem: H.M. Jackson, 'Geradamas, the Celestial Stranger', in *NTS* 27, 1981, 385-394 (with discussion of the previous attempts).
3. 'Das sethianische System nach Nag Hammadi-Handschriften', in *Studia Coptica*, ed. Peter Nagel, (BBA 45), Berlin 1974, 165-173.
4. Carsten Colpe, 'Heidnische, jüdische und christliche Überlieferung in den Schriften aus Nag Hammadi VI', in *Jahrbuch für Antike und Christentum* 20, 1977, 161-170. 'Sethian and Zoroastrian Ages of the World', in *The Rediscovery of Gnosticism*, Proceedings ... Yale, vol. II, 540-552.
5. *Revue des Etudes Augustiniennes*, vol. XXVIII, 1-2, 1981, 3-23.
6. *Den Sethianske Gnosis i lyset af Nag Hammadi teksterne*. (Besvarelse af Københavns Universitets prisspørgsmål i Religionshistorie 1981). Unpublished.
7. The term 'quinity' is borrowed from H.M. Schenke, 'The Phenomenon ...', 603.
8. 'Das sethianische System ...', 170.
9. 'Das sethianische System ...', 170.
10. No parallel in Codex III, pp. 45-48 are missing.
11. Nag Hammadi Codices III,2 and IV,2. *The Gospel of the Egyptians*, edited with translation and commentary by Alexander Böhling and Frederik Wisse in cooperation with Pahor Labib, *NHS* IV, Leiden 1975, 42f.
12. The interchangeability of Barbelo and Iouel is demonstrated in III 44,22 where ΙШΗΛ has taken the place of Barbelo as the male virgin of the great invisible Spirit. On Barbelo and Iouel, see Madalena Scopello, 'Iouel et Barbelo dans le Traite de l'Allogene', in *Colloque International sur les Textes de Nag Hammadi (Quebec 1978)*, ed. Bernard Barc. Biblioteque Copte de Nag Hammadi, Section 'Etudes' 1, Quebec/Louvain 1981, 374-382.
13. The problem of translating the word 'parastasis' in this context is discussed by R. van den Broek, 'Autogenes and Adamas', in *Gnosis und Gnosticismus*, ed. Martin Krause. *NHS* XVII, Leiden 1981, 21. In Irenaios' description of Barbelognostics, based on an unknown version of *Ap.John*, we find in the Latin translation that the four lights were emitted *ad circumstantiam* Autogeni (supported

by the Coptic translation in the NHC II and the BG versions: ⲱϨⲉⲉⲡⲁⲧ⸗), and that Autogenes was emitted *ad representationem* Magni Luminis. Whatever the right translation might be, it doesn't alter the fact that the spiritual seed dwelling in the lights is frequently termed the autogeneis which shows that they are conceived as deriving from an unfolding or differentiation of the divine Autogenes.

14. 'Seth in Gnostic Literature', in *The Rediscovery of Gnosticism*, Proceedings ... Yale, vol. II, 484f.
15. The title 'Son of the Son of Man' is found in *Eugnostos* (NHC III,3 and V,1) and refers without doubt to Seth, although the name doesn't occur in the text. Cf. D.M. Parrott, 'Evidence of Religious Syncretism in Gnostic Texts from Nag Hammadi', in *Religious Syncretism in Antiquity: Essays in Conversation with Geo Widengren*, ed. B.A. Pearson, Missoula/Montana 1975, 179f.
16. The fact that the (preexistent) Gnostics descending from Seth are described both as the autogeneis and the adamases further emphazises the essential identity of Adamas and Autogenes.
17. 'Les quatre illuminateurs ...', 5f.
18. On the problem of chronology I think G. MacRae is right when he suggests that *Apoc. Adam* and *Allogenes* 'belong together a couple of centuries apart'. *The Rediscovery of Gnosticism*, Proceedings ... Yale, vol. II, (Discussion) 679. Note also that Schenke has retracted his earlier hypothesis that *Apoc. Adam* should be regarded as a Gnostic 'Spätprodukt'. *Ibid.* 607.
19. On Sethian cult, see Schenke, 'The Phenomenon ...', 600ff.
20. H. M. Schenke, 'The Phenomenon ...', 612ff.

ATTIS OR OSIRIS?
Firmicus Maternus, *De errore* 22

by Jørgen Podemann Sørensen

With the exception of *Prudentius'* sanguinary account of the *taurobolium* there is perhaps not a more plastic and clear-cut description of a Hellenistic mystery ritual than chapter 22 of the *De errore profanarum religionum*. Among the many vague allusions and hints, and the sometimes badly informed statements of *Firmicus Maternus* this chapter stands out as a more substantial account of the main elements of a ritual performance. It is therefore one of the ironies of our discipline that it has never been clearly and firmly established whether this valuable piece of evidence deals with the cult of Attis or that of Osiris. Hopfner[1] did not include it in *Fontes religionis aegyptiacae*; Turchi[2] quoted it under the headline *De Attidis sacris*; Hepding included it in his collection of sources of the cult of Attis,[3] but with some reservation.[4] To his idea that the all-pervading syncretism of the Hellenistic period may somewhat justify the use of this text to illustrate the Attis cult we shall return later. In the more recent litterature the situation is, I believe, rightly summed up by Cosi[5] as fifty-fifty: an equal number of opinions could be quoted in favour of each of the two gods.

The aim of the present paper is to show that not only the main structure of the ritual described by Firmicus, but each and every single element in it may be identified as *ritus aegyptiacus*. A translation of the text in question may serve as introduction:

§ 1   Let us advance even another *symbolum* in order that the crimes of a mind defiled may become clear; one which must be described point by point to let everyone ascertain the damage done to the law of the divine plan by the perverse imitation of the devil. In a certain night an image is placed on a bier and bemoaned with lamentations in due order over and over again. Next, when they have satisfied themselves with the lamentations prescribed, a light is carried in. Then all those who held lamentation are anointed on their neck by the priest, and when they are duly anointed the priest says in a low and slowly murmuring voice: [in Greek]

> 'Be of good heart, ye mystae of the god now saved; for us too there is salvation from our labours.'

§ 2 Why do you encourage the unhappy to rejoice? Why do you urge deluded people to be happy? What hope, what promise of salvation does your lethal persuasion have for them? Why do you seduce them with mendacious pledges? The death of your god is well known, but his life remains to be seen, and no divine oracle has an answer about his resurrection, and neither does he show himself to people after his death in order that they may believe in him, nor has he forwarded any signs of such an achievement or shown by previous examples that he would do this.

§ 3 You bury an idol, you bemoan an idol, and you produce an idol from the tomb, and in so doing, you miserable one, you rejoice. You liberate your god, you conjoin the lifeless limbs of stone, you arrange the insensible stone. — May your god thank you, may he return your gifts and let you participate in him, that you may die as he dies, that you may live as he lives ...

As it is usual in the patristic literature, Firmicus sees in the theme of the dying and resurrecting god a perverse imitation of the central Christian theme. The religious scene of the Roman empire in the fourth century A.D. is represented in terms of divine and devilish strategies, and the divine plan is constantly threatened by the devil's attempts to bring confusion. Among the most devilish means to distort the divine order are heathen cults like the one described: blasphemously resembling the most central Christian theme, and yet essentially heathen, mythological, and without the historical and eschatological meaning of the death and resurrection of Christ.

The description proper begins with the words

Nocte quadam   *In a certain night*

which do not, of course, offer any means of ascertaining the character or the origin of the ritual. It may mean the night of initiation or a calendrically fixed date, or both. But the ritual takes place at night, and the nightly procedure outlined in the following lines definitely favours Osiris and Egypt:

> *simulacrum in lectico* 　　*an image is placed*
> *supinum ponitur,* 　　　*on a bier*

'supinum' is most likely to imply that the image is a statue lying on its back on the bier, and this is exactly the posture in which an Osiris statue is shown on Egyptian temple reliefs at *Dendera* and *Philae*. Dendera texts give the measures and the materials for such statues.[6]

> *per numeros digestis* 　　*and bemoaned with lamentations*
> *fletibus plangitur* 　　　*over and over again.*

Lamentations form part of the cult of both Attis and Osiris. Firmicus, in this and the following sentence, makes it a point that the wailing is not spontaneous, but follows a prescribed course. Perhaps there is nothing more in this than the general tendency of Christian authors to represent pagan cults as dull routine, but it certainly does not fit the general idea we have of wailing in the cult of Attis. To judge from other sources,[8] an element of spontaneity and even frenzy seems to have been among the more prominent features of the bewailing of Attis. If the passages were meant to account for anything like that, Firmicus would no doubt have taken the opportunity to bring out what would to him and the readers he has in mind be an even greater absurdity.

The ritual bewailing of Osiris is much better known from Egyptian sources. Especially interesting in our context are the so-called *Lamentations of Isis and Nephthys*, extant in two versions on papyri from the Ptolemaic period,[9] and the reliefs and texts in the Ptolemaic and Roman temples of Dendera, Edfu and Philae representing the vigils at the bier of Osiris.[10]

The phrase 'per numeros' suggests a ritual redundancy very similar to what is found in our Egyptian sources. Redundancy is a general feature of not only ancient Egyptian ritual, but of many ritual traditions. In the *Lamentations of Isis and Nephthys*, however, it is indeed a salient feature; over and over again the two wailing women identify themselves as Isis and Nephthys, express their longing for Osiris, and calls him back to his house and his two sisters:

> Come to thine house,
> come to thine house!
> O thou of Heliopolis, come to thine house,
> for thy foes are not.
> O fair Sistrum-player, come to thine house
> that thou mayest see me,

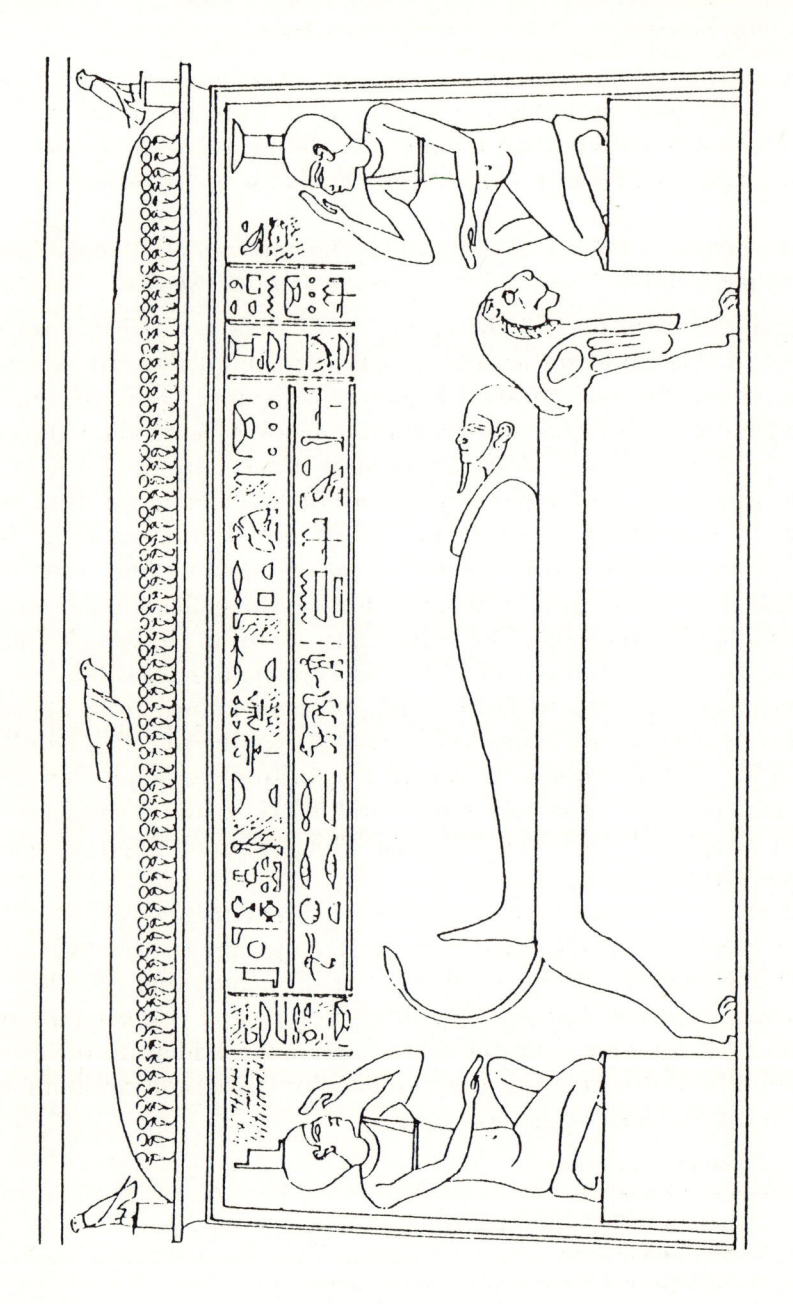

Fig. 1. *Osiris on his bier, bemoaned by Isis and Nephthys.*
(Mariette, op.cit., n. 6)

>   for I am thy sister whom thou lovest,
>   and thou shalt not be parted from me.
>   O fair youth, come to thine house;
>   for a very long while I have not seen thee.
>   My heart grieves for thee,
>   mine eyes search for thee,
>   and I am seeking thee in order to behold thee
>   ...,[11]

Phrases like these are recurrent throughout the lamentations; the long series of invocations, however, not only aims at expressing the grief of the two goddesses, but also, as it appears from the following 'declamation by Nephthys', at restoring Osiris to life:

>   O fair Sovereign, come to thine house
>   and rejoice, for all thy foes are not.
>   Thy two sisters are beside thee
>   as a protection to thy bier,
>   calling upon thee with tears;
>   turn thee about upon thy bier
>   and behold thou the beauteous ones;
>   speak unto us, O Sovereign our lord,
>   that thou mayest drive out all the misery
>   which is in our hearts.
>   ...[12]

In the *Vigils at the bier of Osiris*, likewise a very redundant ritual sequence,[13] lamentations by one or two wailing women identified as Isis and Nephthys occur in most of the twelve vigil hours of both night and day. The ritual of each hour consists of a recital by the priest ($ẖrj-ḥb$), concluding in the announcement of the triumph of Osiris, and a recital by the wailing woman ($ḏrt$). In the latter there is always an element of lamentation, very much in the phraseology already described. As a rule each lamentation will thus be followed, in the next hour, by the priest announcing the triumph of the god.

deinde cum se ficta lamentatione satiaverint,	Next, when they have satified themselves with the lamentations prescribed,

The lamentations, once again, are not spontaneous, but *ficta*, i.e. prescribed or even fictitious. What goes on is not an expression of real grief, but the performance of a ritual. The idea that the participants are satisfied by wailing — or fed up with ritual redundancy — is probably an ironic refinement, from which no conclusion as to the nature of the ritual can be drawn.

> *lumen infertur.* *a light is carried in.*

Bringing light into dark rooms was an essential feature of Egyptian temple ritual. In the daily liturgy, light was first taken into the dark sanctuary, or the sunrays were admitted into the darkness of the inner temple, thus performing the cultic epiphany of the god. From a hidden and potential existence in the primaeval darkness of the sanctuary the god rose to manifest existence — or life. This crucial function of light in a cycle of latent and manifested life, relevant to temple ritual and mortuary cult alike, has been excellently and convincingly shown by Ragnhild Finnestad.[14] The same central Egyptian theme is most probably the background of *Apuleius'* epiphany as the Sun-god, after his initiation into the mysteries of Isis.[15]

In our text, a similar crucial function may be ascribed to the light carried in; it marks the end of a lamentation, of which we have seen that the Egyptian antecedent was also a restoration of Osiris to life; and it is followed up by the announcement that the god is now saved. In order that the *mystae* may participate in the salvation of the god, however, they are first anointed:

> *tunc a sacerdote omnium* Then all those who held
> *qui flebant* lamentation are anointed
> *fauces unguntur* on their neck by the priest,

Anointment is well attested in Egyptian ritual. In the daily liturgy, the cult-statue of the god was anointed,[15] and like most of the rites of the liturgy, this act was said to refresh (*swȝḏ*) the god.[16] The part of the divine body that received the anointment was *ḥȝt*, probably the breast, but in principle *ḥȝt* may denote the whole forepart or upper part of the body.[17] Pictorial representations of one person anointing another show the hand or the oil-jar at the shoulder of the person to be anointed (cf. fig. 2). Considering Egyptian art conventions, however, the upper part of the breast may be meant; for a person is always depicted with shoulders *en face* and the rest in profile. This brings us very close, although perhaps not close enough, to latin *fauces*, throat or neck.

However that may be, anointment played a prominent part in Egyptian ritual; in the *Vigils at the bier of Osiris*, the god was anointed in the

Fig 2. Ankhesenamon anointing Tutankhamon. From the famous throne of Tutankhamon (Howard Carter: The Tomb of Tut-Ankh-Amun. *Vol. 1. London 1923, Pl. 2). The fact that the king wears a pectoral might suggest that the unction was not intended for his shoulder, but rather for his throat or neck.*

second, fourth, fifth, and sixth hour of the day in order that he may prosper (bȝq),[18] triumph (mȝꜥ-ḫrw),[19] and be made festive (sḥb)[20] and ȝḫ,[21] an untranslatable word denoting a state of 'effective being'[22] and commonly used about the blessed dead. These terms are not uncommon as indications of the outcome of Egyptian ritual; they do show, however, that anointment was, in a ritual of Osiris, one of the means to 'save' the god.

In Egyptian mortuary ritual the deceased was regularly identified with Osiris; the very aim of many rites was to make the deceased participate in the regeneration of Osiris. Private individuals would thus, once they were dead, be ritually treated very much as was Osiris in the temple. They would, among other things, be anointed during the ritual of embalming, often with express reference to their participation in the regeneration of Osiris.[23]

In the Hellenistic mystery ritual described by Firmicus Maternus, private individuals, but living ones, were likewise made to participate in the regeneration or the 'salvation' of Osiris. Anointment was the ritual marking of their share in divine regeneration.

quibus perunctis,	and when they are duly anointed
sacerdos hoc	the priest says in a low and
lento murmure susurrat:	slowly murmuring voice:

There is not, to my knowledge, any Egyptian evidence for this style of reciting a ritual text. The current terms in connection with the Osiris rituals in the month of Choiak, ꜥš (shout) and njs (call),[24] rather suggest that the rituals are pronounced in a loud voice. There may, of course, have been passages in Egyptian ritual texts which were to be recited in a low voice, but it is important to notice that the passage here involved has the character of a Hellenistic conclusion drawn from Egyptian premises; if its recitation does not conform to *ritus aegyptiacus*, this needs not disturb us.

Anyway the whole sentence is perhaps more of a satire than a description. The relative which introduces it is a pedantic and redundant reference to the immediately preceeding sentence as if to bring out the tediousness of a long and meticulous ritual procedure. This impression is strengthened by the use of *murmur* with the verb *susurro*; the two words may denote very much the same low, humming or buzzing sound characteristic of (Roman) prayer or ritual. The sentence seems thus designed to exhibit the lengthy and tedious character of the ritual, and its basis in direct observation may be very little.

ϑαρρεῖτε μύσται τοῦ ϑεοῦ σεσωσμένου; ἔσται γὰρ ἡμῖν ἐκ πόνων σωτηρία.	'Be of good heart, ye mystae of the god now saved; for us too there is salvation from our labours.'

These words, addressed to the *mystae*, represent the Hellenistic soteriological reinterpretation of the mystery of Osirian regeneration. The regeneration of the god is seen to have a bearing on the salvation of the particular group gathered to participate in the mystery. In ancient Egypt the destiny of the individual was, in funerary texts since the end of the Old Kingdom, closely tied to the Osirian regeneration scheme. Each individual deceased person was, in the funerary texts buried with him, identified with Osiris, and in fact the passages quoted above from the *Lamentations of Isis and Nephthys* are from a version copied for the benefit of a certain Tentruty to be buried with her.[25] One might say that Osiris was already from the end of the Old Kingdom *exemplar* of individual salvation. As far as we know, however, he was so in funerary rituals and funerary texts, not in initiatory rites for private, living people. And the salvation in question was not ἐκ πόνων σωτηρία. It was a matter of securing, for an individual person and in an individual family, that regeneration of life which was the rythm of nature itself.

The following passages, § 2, no longer describe the ritual, but rather aim at bringing out the difference between the heathen mysteries and Christian history. The heathen god is nothing but a mythical prototype, whereas the life, death, and resurrection of Christ took place in history. Interesting as they are in their own right we shall, however, leave these passages out of consideration for our present purpose.

§ 3, although stylistically continuous with the preceeding paragraph, again has decisive information about the content of the ritual. It does not simply resume the description interrupted by § 2, but rather goes on to exhibit, in a polemical way, the broader context and meaning of the ritual:

Tu idolum sepelis, *idolum plangis,*	*You bury an idol,* *you bemoan an idol,*

> *idolum de sepultura profers,* *you produce an idol from the tomb,*

The ritual burial of Osiris is known since the 12th dynasty in Egypt, and Ptolemaic temples had rooms called the 'tomb of Osiris'.[26] The festival calendar of Dendara[27] twice mentions Osiris resting in his sarcophagus, and it is also clear from this text that he goes forth from his coffin; this was ritually enacted by taking his statue out for a procession.

The rites described by Firmicus in § 1 and resumed in part by the words 'idolum plangis' may have belonged to such a context, although rites performed by small mystery communities could not, of course, be expected to meet Ptolemaic standards. In Firmicus' scheme, the lamentation is connected with the funeral of the idol and joy, as we shall see in the next sentence, with taking the idol out of the tomb:

> *et miser cum haec feceris, gaudes.* *and in so doing, you miserable one, you rejoice.*

The joy here alluded to corresponds to $\vartheta\alpha\rho\rho\epsilon\tilde{\iota}\tau\epsilon\ \mu\acute{\upsilon}\sigma\tau\alpha\iota$ in § 1, and it would thus seem that Firmicus is not describing a new ritual sequence, but commenting in a more abstract manner on the structure and meaning of the one already described. — Lamentations followed by jubilation is one of the attested characteristics of the cult of Attis.[28] There is, however, no obstacle to regarding it as *ritus aegyptiacus*; Egyptian ritual texts represent the shift from lamentation to joy in the cult of Osiris clearly and directly. In the *Vigils at the bier of Osiris* it is the wailing woman who, at the end of her lamentations, announces joy and jubilation,[29] and in the same text Isis is said to exult from love of Osiris.[30] Allusions to the joy and jubilation to follow the regeneration of Osiris are likewise found in the *Lamentations of Isis and Nephthys*.[31]

> *Tu deum tuum liberas,* *You liberate your god,*

These words are perhaps best taken to refer, in a polemical way, to the current Hellenistic idea of *salvator salvandus*, a god whose mythological fate is a soteriological paradigm, but who needs salvation himself. — And the poor heathen has to do the work of salvation for his saviour, to liberate his god while himself in need of liberation. The concept of liberation, as applied to the ritual, is probably nothing more than a resumption of $\dot{\epsilon}\kappa\ \pi\acute{o}\nu\omega\nu\ \sigma\omega\tau\eta\rho\acute{\iota}\alpha$ in § 1.

tu iacentia lapidis	*you conjoin the lifeless*
membra componis,	*limbs of stone,*

This sentence is the main argument for an Osirian interpretation. The dismemberment of Osiris and the subsequent gathering of his limbs by Isis is a feature of Egyptian mythology unparalleled in the religions of Western Asia and Europe.

A passage in the longer version of the *Lamentations of Isis and Nephthys* associates this motif with the wailing of the two sisters:

> They reassemble thy limbs for thee with mourning,
> seeking to take care of thy corpse.[32]

The reassembling of the limbs of Osiris is here seen as the result of the mourning of the two sisters. Although this fits the ritual structure outlined by Firmicus very well, his particular mention of *lapidis membra* points to a more dramatic reenactment of the reassembling of Osiris' limbs. — During the festival of Choiak such a dramatic performance took place. It is described, not in its entire ritual context, but in certain directions for the moulding of an image of Osiris, reproduced on the walls of an Osiris chapel in Dendera.[33] The image, which is called Sokaris (in the Dendera rituals this god is often identified or intermingled with Osiris) is made of various substances and moulded into a form. The various ingredients have to be carefully measured in fourteen parts of the divine body:

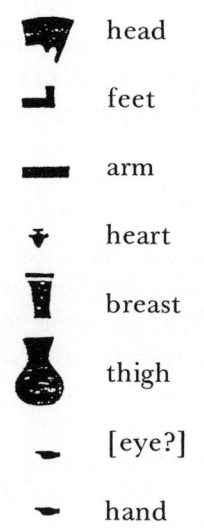

- head
- feet
- arm
- heart
- breast
- thigh
- [eye?]
- hand

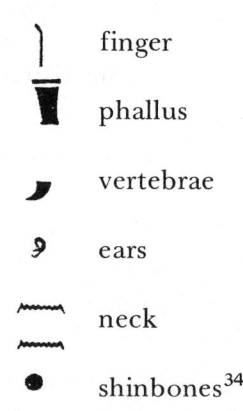

⎤	finger
𓂸	phallus
𖡄	vertebrae
𖡅	ears
〰〰	neck
●	shinbones[34]

The preparation of the image of Sokaris was thus a ritual reenactment of the gathering of the limbs of Osiris. The ingredients measured and brought together in these receptacles were no *lapidis membra*, but the Dendera text shows that the reassembling of the divine limbs *was* dramatically performed in Egypt.

If Firmicus is really describing a ritual where *lapidis membra* were actually manipulated, then it is different from the one described in Dendera, but clearly and undoubtedly Egyptian and Osirian.

tu insensibile   *you arrange the*
corrigis saxum ...   *insensible stone ...*

This last descriptive statement of the chapter may be taken as a continuation or even a repetition of the preceding sentence. 'Saxum' most probably refers to the *lapidis membra*; 'corrigis' might be taken to mean that the reassembled divine body is somehow raised. There would be a clear parallel of this in the *Vigils*, where Horus and Isis are said to 'raise the god in his shape (*jrw.f*).[35] 'Corrigis', however, may mean nothing more that 'you arrange', and in that case the whole sentence is nothing but another exhibition of the absurdity of what was already told. Stylistically this interpretation is the more satisfactory one, since the sentence would thus provide a transition to the following purely polemical statements.

In conclusion, one last point must be made. We have seen that although we have not been able to point to *one* ancient Egyptian ritual as the prototype of the mystery described by Firmicus, our specific interpretation of it in terms of *ritus aegyptiacus* has yielded a consistent account of its meaning. This was made posible, above all, by the rich sources of ancient Egyptian ritual tradition; and the freedom one still has, admittedly, to believe that this chapter deals with Attis seems to me mainly due to the fact that so little is know of *ritus phrygicus*. — To allow for an all-pervading syncretism, which would make this text illustrative of the mysteries of Osiris and Attis alike, as Hepding tended to do, means to interpret it in terms of generalized Hellenistic concepts only; and it will then no longer illustrate the process of syncretism. Progress in our understanding of the Hellenistic process depends on specific studies of meaning and shifts of meaning.

NOTES:

1. Hopfner, Th.: *Fontes Historiae Religionis Aegyptiacae*. Bonnae 1922-25.
2. Turchi, N.: *Fontes historiae mysteriorum*. 1930. Text no. 269, p. 239.
3. Hepding, H.: *Attis, seine Mythen und sein Kult*. Giessen 1903, p. 50.
4. *ibid.*, p. 167.
5. cf. D.M. Cosi in *La soteriologia dei culti orientali nell'impero Romano*. Leiden 1982, (EPRO 42), p. 489. Cosi himself, however, definitely favours Attis.
6. Mariette, A.: *Denderah*. Paris 1870, vol. IV, pl. 88 sqq.
7. *loc.cit.*
8. Hepding, *op.cit.*, n. 3, p. 40 (Arnobius); p. 158 sqq.
9. P. Berlin 3008, cf. Faulkner in *Melanges Maspero*. I, Cairo 1935-38, p. 337-348. — Faulkner, R.O.: *The papyrus Bremmer-Rhind*. (Bibliotheca aegyptiaca; 3), Bruxelles 1933 (transl. by Faulkner in *Journal of Egyptian Archaeology*; 22, p. 121 sqq.).
10. Junker, H.: *Die Stundenwachen in den Osirismysterien*. (Denkschr. d. kais. Ak. d. Wiss. in Wien, Phil.-hist. Kl., Band 54) Wien 1910.
11. Faulkner's transl. in *Melanges Maspero* I, p. 339.
12. *ibid.*, p. 341.
13. Moret, A.: *Mysteres Egyptiens*. Paris 1923, p. 23 sq.
14. Finnestad, R.: *Image of the world and symbol of the creator*. Wiesbaden 1985, esp. p. 111 sq.
15. Apuleius, *Metam*. XI, 24.
16. P. Berlin 3055, 30, 8 sqq. — cf. Moret, A.: *Le rituel du culte divin journalier en Egypte*. Paris 1902.
17. *ibid.* 31, 9-10; cf. Wb. III, 19.
18. Junker, *Stundenwachen*, p. 40.
19. *ibid.*, p. 50.
20. *ibid.*, p. 53.
21. *ibid.*, p. 58.

22. on *akh*, cf. Englund, G.: *Akh*. Uppsala 1978 (Boreas; 11).
23. cf. Sauneron, S.: *Rituel de l'Embaumement*. Le Caire 1952. Transl. Goyon, J.-Cl.: *Rituel funeraires de l'ancienne Egypte*. Paris 1972. §§ I-IV, pp. 42-50.
24. cf. Barguet, Paul: *Le papyrus N. 3176 (S) du Musee du Louvre*. Le Caire 1962, p. 16, line 11 of the papyrus; p. 21, line 12 of the papyrus.
25. cf. *Melanges Maspero* I, p. 338.
26. cf. Schäfer, H.: *Die Mysterien des Osiris in Abydos unter König Sesostris III*. Lpz. 1904; Cauville, S.: *Edfou*. Le Caire 1984, p. 42.
27. Parker, *Calendars of Egypt*, p. 59 sq.
28. Hepding, *Attis*, p. 165 sq.
29. Junker, *Stundenwachen*, p. 37, cf. p. 71 sqq. and p. 111.
30. *ibid.*, p. 61.
31. e.g. P. Bremmer-Rhind 13, 11.
32. *ibid.* 11, 7 sq.
33. cf. Chassinat, E.: *Le mystere d'Osiris au mois de Khoiak*. Le Caire 1966-68, p. 493 sqq.
34. *loc.cit.* — cf. also p. 57 sq.
35. Junker, *Stundenwachen*, p. 93.

THE GATEWAYS OF JUDAISM
FROM SIMON THE JUST TO RABBI AKIBA

by Karin Weinholt

Sources and Problems

It may seem a luxury to start to make comments on sources and problems, when you are going to make a brief sketch of a period in Jewish history. All the same I shall do so, realizing the problems bound to parts of the material.

Jewish Hebrew and Aramaic sources from the Second Temple period until Talmudic times are divided into three sectors: the Written Law (Scripture), the Oral Law transmitted in the rabbinic literature, the Apocrypha and the Pseudepigrapha. The Apocrypha and the Pseudepigrapha present their own problems which will not be discussed here, I only want to point to their belonging to Jewish tradition during the period in question. The Rabbis about whom we are going to talk, were fully aware of the Jewish and non-canonical character of the Apocrypha, to some extent of the Pseudepigrapha, too.

The Oral Law includes different collections, the main compilations being the Mishna, the Tosefta, the Palestinian and the Babylonian Talmudim and the various Midrashim. We know the dates of the redaction of these collections in their written forms, just as we know that their contents were transmitted orally for centuries before. I shall point out some characteristics of the transmission, arguing that they point to the reliability of the tradition.

The statements in the rabbinic traditions are mostly named: Rabbi so and so said in the name of Rabbi so and so. As tradition is transmitted, it grows. Generally it is expressly mentioned in the tradition, when additions, reformulations and adaptions are made. To a modern reader it is astonishing to see to which extent rabbinic teachers and pupils were able to remember all the details.

From the traditions it appears, that some scholars and disciples kept records or notebooks. The notebooks were at first meant for private use. Some Sages warn against written records, they consider the written form to be the privilege of — the Scripture. Nevertheless, from Rabbi Akiba we hear about proper written collections of traditions. Akiba himself made preparations to classify and write down the material of the Mishnah. Rabbi Meir, one of the disciples of Akiba, continued his masters work. Rabbi Meir's fundamental decisions are the basis of Rabbi Yehudah ha-Nasi's Mishnah.

Some of the vast traditions are anonymous. They are called *stam Mishnayot*. These anonymous rules, regulations or stories are considered old, that is: at least tannaitic. As to them the rabbinic rule states: they are following Rabbi Meir in accordance with Rabbi Akiba, *stam Mishnah k^e Rabbi Meir d^e Rabbi Akiba*.

Thus both the anonymous and the named tradition admit fixpoints for dating. The first name of the named traditions is that of Simon the Just, high priest and scribe during the reign of Alexander (or his successors).[1] From this Hellenistic period the named traditions are few, their numbers increase greatly from the Roman reign onwards. About the beginning of the Christian era the schools of Hillel and Shammai become normative in Jewish tradition. Akiba often takes an attitude in accordance with Hillel or the school of Hillel, just as the hermeneutic method of Akiba is an unfolding of the methodic rules of Hillel.

The teachings of the schools of Hillel and Shammai mean an enormous development in tradition and of traditions. When a matter is discussed, teachers and students can go back to the schools of Hillel and Shammai. It was the school of Hillel that became normative to Jewry. But it is characteristic that the traditions transmit the full discussions. The point of view that was rejected by the majority of the Sages, is handed down, too. The rejected point of view still has its chance in later generations.

Another criterion for dating the tradition is the comparison of sources. One Talmudic source may be confirmed by another, and Talmudic sources may be confirmed by non-Talmudic. The non-Talmudic sources are many, some of them having just as direct a relevance to the period in question as the rabbinic literature, for instance the Jewish literature in Greek with names as Josephus and Philo, and we could go on with the Apocrypha and the Pseudepigrapha already mentioned, the Qumran-literature, the New Testament, the Church Fathers, the Greek and Latin historians and so on.

The reason why I have made a stop at the rabbinic literature is the assumption on the part of many Christian biblical scholars, that the rabbinic literature is an uncertain source. I have argued the opposite point of view. Moreover, precise dating or not, the Oral Law reflects Jewish life during centuries. Whether halakah or haggadah, all aspects of life are represented.

Under the main theme I shall talk about the regulations of the Sages called the fence of the Torah. Here I might add that not all but a large part of the tradition — and both the legislative material, halakah, and the narrative, haggadah — are derived from the study of Scripture, When the Sages met a problem of current interest, they studied Scripture. In the Mishnah, in the middle of legislative discussions, you may find the most beatiful and devotional interpretations. Take this example from the halakah, an example which also gives the character of the legislative material into the bargain:

> 'This is my God, and I will glorify Him' (Ex. 15,2). Rabbi Ishmael says: 'Can a being of flesh and blood glorify his maker? No, the interpretation is: I shall glorify him with precepts, I shall make before him a beautiful lulab, a beautiful tabernacle, beautiful fringes, beautiful phylacteries.' Abba Shaul says: 'I shall imitate him. Just as he is merciful and compassionate, so be thou merciful and compassionate' (Mekilta, Shirah, ch. 3)

The point of reference in a discussion may be Scripture. Or it may be historical events. Especially during the Roman history of Palestine historical events provoke halakah and haggadah. We must admit that it is not always an easy task to point out *the* historical event. But to create a picture of the Jewish history, you have to take the risk of pointing out events.

The main problem for the student of rabbinic literature, however, particularly when the aim is to outline the history and its men, is the abundant and disparate character of the material. You have not followed the discussions of a problem or sketched the history to a high degree of possibility, until you have found all the notes and tiny remarks on it scattered in the vast literature. And even then you have not finished, it is only then the comparative work with the non-Talmudic sources begins.

Of further introductory remarks I shall hint at the relationship between Jewry in Palestine and Jewry in the Diaspora in Late Antiquity. How was the Written Law understood and used in the Diaspora, how was the Oral Law looked upon? Was the Pharisaic movement powerful enough to extend its regulations and traditions to the Jews dispersed in the Babylonian and the Greco-Roman areas and even beyond these borders? The answers given by modern scholars are not unanimous. One thing I find certain; the Jews of the Diaspora looked to the Jews of the Holy Land for guidance. It is characteristic, that the Palestinian schools in Talmudic times enjoy a reputation, which remains a long time after it rightly ought to have passed to the Babylonian schools. Besides, the circumstances in Palestine during the Hellenistic-Roman period were not so very different from the circumstances in the Diaspora.

Finally: in the following I shall concentrate on the main stream in Judaism in the period discussed, e.g. Pharisaism and its successor Rabbinism. I am fully aware of the diversified society of Palestinian Jewry during these centuries. But I consider Pharisaism as the dynamic force in Judaism, the force that was responsible for the survival of a Judaism in dynamic development in spite of the catastrophies of the First and Second Revolt against Rome. This consideration corresponds to the picture won from the rabbinic literature and from Josephus among other sources.

Alexander the Great and Simon the Just. An Approach to Hellenism

With Simon the Just we are situated in Palestine in the Hellenistic era. It is a Palestine, which has been under Persian rule and has enjoyed royal mercy as well as experienced the already known lot of the oppressed. During the Persian period Nehemiah and later Ezra were sent from the Persian court with royal permission to rebuild the walls of Jerusalem and to give the Law of Moses the same status as the law of the Persian king; the latter event is described in Ezra ch. 7.

As early as during Persian rule Greek mercenaries and merchants made their way through Palestine. From the fifth and the fourth centuries objects of different kinds are found in Palestine, which bear witness to Hellenistic culture and religion. It is not with a sudden blow that Hellenism shows itself on the Judean stage, when Jerusalem opens her gates to Alexander the Great. But it is true that from the time of Alexander it happens with a force and to an amount hitherto unknown.

Jewish legend found a most beloved topic in the meeting between the Jewish deputies sent out to surrender the Holy City, and the Macedonian king. In Jewish literature from the Middle Ages and onwards Alexander Hamukdon is characterized as the great hero, who wants to protect and defend the Jews and the Jewish religion from all enemies. In rabbinic sources (Scolion to Megillat Ta'anit; B.T. Yoma 69 a) we are told, how Simon the Just met Alexander the Great — the high priest invites the conqueror into the city, shows him the Temple, and the incredible happens: Alexander bends his knees to the God of Israel.

It is of interest to look at the picture drawn of the Macedonian king: he is represented as the Godfearer, he who honours the one, true God, bends his knees to this mighty power of life, without taking the last step and becoming a proselyte. It is interesting, too, to consider the attitude of Simon.

Simon might be looked upon as a renegade, but in Jewish tradition it never occurs. We meet him as the proud Jew, conscious of representing the highest religion and faith. He takes the stranger's hand and shows him the wonders of God, e.g. he leads the gentile to the truth of life. In the Mishna tractate Pirke Abot it is stated that Simon 'was among the last men of the great assembly', an institution from the time and work of Ezra, continued in the great Sanhedrin in Greek-Roman time. And Simon is quoted saying: 'On three things the world stands: on the Torah, on Worship, and on acts of loving-kindness' (Pirke Abot 1, 2).

The Talmudic informations correspond to those of Josephus (Ant. XIII, 43ff., 157ff.; compare Eccl. 50, 1-21). Thus — in spite of the problems of dating: does Simon belong to the end of the fourth century or to the end of the third century? — we may use Simon as a symbolic figure, characterizing the well educated Jew, who is proud of his tradition and openminded towards strangers, among these strangers with a Hellenistic background, maybe even especially interested in the Hellenistic culture.

It is worth noticing, that the figure of Simon the Just belongs to a period in the history of Palestine after the reformation of Ezra and of other Jews inspired from the exile. In the story of Ezra you might find indications of narrowmindedness, that narrowmindedness with which the legalism of Judaism is often identified. It is obvious, that what Nehemiah did physically: built up the walls of Jerusalem, Ezra did spiritually: he formed and reformed the walls of Judaism. But the aim was not to create narrowmindedness, it was to save Judaism from ruin. During certain periods in the history of the Jewish people, Ezra's walls created narrow rooms, during others, however, they created the possibility and reality of walls with wide open gateways.

It is wellknown that Hellenism influenced various Oriental cultures, and that the Oriental cultures made the reverse movement. Hellenism became the intermingling of Greece and the Orient. Judaism brought something of its own to the meeting. However, as to the Jewish elements it might be better to talk about interaction, not intermingling.

Greek authors from the fourth and third century B.C.E. describe the Jews as a people of philosophers.[2] They point to the faith in the one God, to Moses as the legislator, and they mention the moral regulations. Some of these authors supposed, that Pythagoras did learn not only from Egypt and Chaldea, but from Jewish wisdom, too. Correspondingly Philo argues that the Greek sages had learned their loftier conceptions of God from Moses. Both were probably wrong, though the arguments are not absurd. In his work against the antisemite Apion (1, 22) Josephus recounts the Jewish rule, later found in the Mishnah (M. Terumot 8, 4ff.), that drinking water which stood uncovered is prohibited. Josephus refers to a Greek writer of the third century, who claims that Pythagoras adopted this custom from the Jews. — It should be noticed that in Roman times the references to the Jews tend towards antisemitism.[3]

We are not able to controle the individual example. We know, that when Simon the Just or his like opened the gates to Alexander the Great, Greek language and ideas crossed the borders. As already mentioned: something crossed back the other way. The Hermetic literature might be used as an example. It is plausible, that a connexion exists between Judaism and Gnosticism. As to the Hermetic literature we can point to Poimandres, and to the description of creation there. We may conclude that the story of creation from Genesis has found its way to the Hellenistic world. Maybe through the Godfearers (or proselytes) who listened to the reading of the Law in the synagogues of the Diaspora.

Discussing interaction the Jewish ideas of death must be mentioned. It is often taught that the Jewish thoughts about death in the era of the Second Temple were basically influenced by foreign and among them Greek ideas. However, it should not be forgotten that the Pharisees believed in a soul or an inward man, and at the same time taught the physical resurrection from the dead. They believed in a paradise of the souls, and at the same time taught the judgement of every man at the resurrection of the bodies. Which of these ideas — if any — were Greek? We might also ask: are there Greek ideas in the Jewish stories of the creation of man, or were they Jewish from their origin?

Josephus' recount of Eliezer ben Jair's speech to the rebels at the top of Masada shows the interaction; or it points to the open roads along which thoughts of life and death were always walking. Be it the Indians, whom Eliezer explicitly mentions, be it the Jews, who in the actual situation are going to choose suicide as the alternative to bondage and endless sufferings — in spite of all differences they count on eternal life, the survival of inward man.

Whatever happened, when the rabbis discussed these themes, they were convinced of their genuine Jewishness. The same is true of their teachings of this world and the world to come and the like. This, however, does not mean that they closed their eyes to the interaction. What they believed was that the one and true God held life and death, the whole world and all worlds, in his hand. And in believing this they knew, that all the words and expressions that man uses describing his faith, are but human and earthly pictures.

Discussing interaction in Palestine during the Second Temple period, the existence of the Greek cities with their independent organization cannot be overlooked. As to Palestine we know about a great number of these independent cities on the Philistine and Phoenician coast, moreover in the east and north-east of Palestine, and also in the interior of Palestine Hellenistic cities were found (Tiberias, Sephoris, Scytopolis/Bet Shean, Antipatris Samaria, Neopolis, Marissa). The mainpart of the population in these cities, be it outside or inside Palestine, was non-Jewish. However, it was not entirely non-Jewish. Interaction was unavoidable. Or rather it was natural.

True, the Maccabees revolted against the Greek oppression. But it was the religious abominences which were to be removed. The Hasmonean kings and high priests adopted Hellenistic administration, for instance. And administrational systems taken over from strangers were not the only heritage from the Greek, which was not considered an abomination during the Second Temple period.

Hellenism and Judaism. Confrontation and Inspiration

To provide an illumination of everyday life in Palestine during the Hellenistic-Roman period, we may outline some situations:

a Jewish housewife goes to the marketplace to buy a pot. She finds a good one and in the wanted size. But it has some pictures on its sides, and this poses the question: do the pictures make the pot prohibited for use in a Jewish house?

Another illumination: a Jewish houseowner is going to repair a wall, and he looks for suitable stones. He finds some which seem to be discarded. But they happen to have been used in a Hermeticum, a place which was holy to idolaters. Can he use them in his house?

Or: another Jewish person finds a vase in a ditch, he brings it to his private garden as an ornament. But if the vase has been part of an idol, of a statue which was worshipped by an idolater, is he then allowed to use it?

To all such questions the rabbis gave their answers, thus forming the Oral Law.

I shall repeat that I am aware of the abundant character of Judaism during the period. But I am convinced that the Pharisees and their successors were everywhere, and that they were popular; they were the men to whom you came for a decision in cases as those just outlined. This position they inherited from Simon the Just and Antigonos from Socho, the disciple of Simon. It was a position which grew through the period of the socalled pairs (*zugot*), of whom Hillel and Shammai became the most famous. Through teachers as Rabbi Yohanan ben Zakkai and Rabban Gamliel the Second the advising activity and guidance binds together Jerusalem and Jabne, just as it leads Israel safely through the catastrophies during the reign of Trajan and of Hadrian, now with Rabbi Akiba and his disciples as the outstanding Sages.

The rabbis were believers. They were intellectuals, too. But first and foremost they were men of everyday life. They did not hide in the schoolhouse, their place of work was also the marketplace, the street, the field.

The teachings of these men constitutes a fence of the Torah. The commandments of the law of Moses are recognized as divine, but as bound up with life of the past, too. Life as it unfolds itself in later generations still and forever belongs to the area of the divine commandments. But to be able to follow these commandments in later generations, it is necessary to regulate. The fence of the Torah is this regulation.

I know very well that it is not until Maimonides that one might define the Oral Law in words like those just used. The Pharisees before 70 C.E. and the rabbis thereafter would rather talk about the regulations as a measure against violations of the Torah given to Moses on Mount Sinai; compare the word 'fence'. Nevertheless, an awareness of time that passes by can be found in hints and attitudes of the Sages of Late Antiquity.

The rabbis make regulations, intended to be observed in Jewish life. In Christian tradition this is considered a yoke. The word 'yoke' is in fact used by the Sages about the regulations. But we should remember what a yoke is: it helps you to carry the heaviest burdens, so that they are not felt that heavy.

> 'Come unto me, all ye that labour and are heavy laden, and I will give you rest. Take my yoke upon you, and learn of me; ... For my yoke is easy, and my burden is light' (Matt. 11, 28-30).

These are words which any great rabbi can speak.

By the way, it is characteristic that no penalties are set up for violations of regulations given by the Sages. Whereas penalties, earthly and heavenly, are prescribed, if the Written Law is violated. The fence of the Torah is established to your relief.

To turn to the questions which we imagine were put to the rabbis: they deal with the case of *'avodah zarah*, idolatry. If a Jew violates the commandments against idolatry, it is a most serious crime. The fence set up around these commandments might be supposed to be like strong, unpenetrable walls. In a way they are. It is completely forbidden to use and take advantage of an idol. *If* it is an idol. But as to this the discussions repeatedly run forwards and backwards. If the rabbinic discussion leaves any doubt, the object is prohibited. But that Jews could walk without trouble and too much care in the Greek streets, could go to the theatre, or go bathing in a Roman bath, you will understand from the following passage in the Mishnah:

> Proclos the son of a philosopher asked Rabban Gamliel in Acco when he was bathing in a bath, where there was a statue of Aphrodite; he said to him: 'It is written in your Law: 'And then shall cleave naught of the devoted thing to your hand', why bathest thou in the bath of Aphrodite?' He made reply to him: 'One may not answer in the bath.'[4] And when Rabban Gamliel came out he said to him: 'I came not within her limits, she came within my limits. People do not say: 'The bath is built as an adornment for Aphrodite', but 'Aphrodite is made as an adornment for the bath'. Further: 'If they were to give thee much money, thou wouldst not enter before thy idolatrous service naked or while suffering from a discharge, nor micturate before her; and yet this statue stands at the mouth of the gutter and all the people micturate in front of her! It is only said 'their gods',[5] e.g. what is treated as a god is prohibited, but what is not treated as a god is permitted' ('Avodah Zarah 3, 4).

Rabban Gamliel is Gamliel the Second, the successor of Yohanan ben Zakkai in Jabne. He is known as a stern, severe teacher and leader, who wanted to bring about a unification of Jewry after the fall of the Temple. In the bath of Acco we are led through the gateways of *his* strong walls.

We should note, of course, that the subject of the discussion is not pictures of the Roman Emperor. Just as idols treated as idols are prohibited, so pictures of the Emperor treated as such are prohibited to Jews; and pictures of the Emperor are hardly considered ornamental.[6]

Tradition is a conception bound to the past. But if the tradition is a living one, it is bound to the present, too. Simon the Just — this symbolic figure — understood how Law and life are inseparably connected. This is the attitude of the Sages of the period.

When in a lecture you are surveying the chain of Sages from Simon to Akiba, it has to be selective. And I can only hint at the hardships of Jewish history, as for instance the persecutions of the Pharisees by the Hasmoneans John Hyrkanos and Alexander Jannai; for a quarter of a century the Pharisees were excluded from the Sanhedrin, many of them were executed, a larger number fled to the Diaspora. During the reign of queen Alexandra Salome they were progressing by leaps and bounds. The advent of the Romans in Syria-Palestine does not stop their growth, on the contrary they now get politically involved, sending deputies to the Roman masters, thus representing their views of possible and impossible, desirable and undesirable leaders of the Jewish territory. During the reign of Herod the Great, when the influence of the Sanhedrin is minimized, the Pharisaic schools flourish, the teachers and teachings taking deep roots in the people, roots which lie firmly in the ground during all the shocking events of the period of the procurators. Until at last they prove themselves able to make green shoots in spite of the catastrophies of the years 66-73 and 132-135 — these catastrophies being anticipated and followed by persecutions and massacres led by Hellenistic citizens or by the Roman force.

I have mentioned the pairs (*zugot*), of whom Hillel and Shammai are outstanding. The anecdotes told about the two are numerous. Hillel, the Diaspora Jew who came to study in the famous schools of the Holy Land, is depicted as a man of a kind and open temperament, the ideal teacher who follows the pupil, though he in reality leads him. Some of the wellknown stories are about a gentile, asking Hillel to teach him Torah immediately or make him a high priest, on which condition the gentile will convert to Judaism. Though Hillel does not accept the requirements, he gently leads the gentile to Judaism. Exactly the opposite thing is told about Shammai who throws this impertinent and foolish gentile out.

Listening to these stories we might get a picture of openness on the side of Hillel and strictness on the side of Shammai. The conclusion is tempting: some of the teachers in Israel were really openminded while others were schoolmasters with narrow views and austere morals; and we shall probably be right — but not in the case of Shammai. Both Hillel and Shammai can be severe in details of legislation, and both of them have the outlook, which includes the poor, the unlearned, the stranger. The Pharisaic view of the crown of the Torah, which may be gained by anyone, fits Shammai as well as Hillel. Was it not Shammai, who said: 'Receive all men with a kindly countenance!' (Pirke Abot 1, 15).

However, the popularity of Hillel and his school was unique. He possessed a flexibility in attitude, in hermeneutics as well as in legislative work, which made his decisions live on. His flexibility was a political attitude, too. It is characteristic that from the hillelites a Yohanan ben Zakkai goes forth, the rabbi who did not open the gates of Jerusalem to the conqueror like Simon the Just, but who according to the legend was carried out in a coffin to meet the conqueror, when that conqueror's name was Vespasian. In some traditions Rabbi Yohanan is called 'one of the Emperor's friends'.

Yohanan ben Zakkai renewed life for Jews and Judaism through the academy of Jabne. He is a Sage, whom Jewish tradition places on a par with Abraham and Moses. His reforms have reference to that core, which is the essence of the conversation with Rabbi Joshua, told in Abot d^e-Rabbi Nathan (1, 2):

> Once as Rabban Johanan ben Zakkai was coming forth from Jerusalem, Rabbi Joshua followed after him and beheld the Temple in ruins. 'Woe unto us!' Rabbi Joshua cried, 'that this, the place where the iniquities of Israel were atoned for, is laid vaste!' 'My son,' Rabban Johanan said to him, 'be not grieved; we have another atonement as effective as this. And what is it? It is acts of lovingkindness, as it is said: For I desire mercy and not sacrifice.'

The attitude of Rabbi Yohanan is further more, that lovingkindness flows from the study of Torah.

This great man is reported to have had close contacts to Rome! To Vespasian and Titus he proved to be an ally, moreover tradition hints to a connection with Hadrian. No matter how legendary these relationships are, they testify to Yohanan as a man of common sense and to his ability as a practical politician. When Rabbi Akiba saw Simon bar Kochba (Koseba), he said: 'This is the king Messiah!' Many of the hillelites protested, Rabbi Yohanan ben Torta said: 'Akiba, grass will sprout through your cheeks ere the son of David comes.' And Rabbi Yohanan ben Zakkai said: 'Hark! the voice of Hadrian Caesar slaying eighty thousand myriads in Bethar!' (J.T. Ta'anit ch. IV).

The last years of Trajan's reign and the hadrianic era were unhappy years in Israel. Most of the rabbis who were the spiritual and often the political leaders of the people, had learned the lesson from the year seventy, and they tried to make the best of the worst, though in different ways. It may be characteristic, that the shammaites were much more reserved in their attitude towards Rome. They did not believe that good times were coming, when Nerva altered the *fiscus judaicus* in a way which might indicate a promise from the Emperor to the Jews of Palestine as to the fulfillment of their highest desire: the rebuilding of the Temple. The shammaites were right, Trajan gave up the matter. But Yohanan and the other hillelites were right, too: without intercourse and negotiation with open minds and hearts, there was no future for the minority.

In the aftermath of the Second Revolt the Jews were met with Hadrian's prohibitions and persecutions. Nevertheless, the Roman ruler could still be looked upon as a parallel to the great Alexander, who was greeted by the Jewish high priest:

> Hadrian said to Rabbi Joshua: 'Great indeed must be the lamb, Israel, that can exist among seventy wolves.' Rabbi Joshua replied: 'Great is the shepherd who rescues and protects her' (Tanhuma, Toledot, 45 a-45 b).

Practical politics, indeed, but theology at the same time. The famous Akiba shows the duplicity. Akiba was no shammaite, and he had confidence in negotiations with Rome, just as he might have believed in promises concerning the alteration of the fiscus.[7] He was among the four Sages sent to Rome to Domitian in 95 C.E. Besides Akiba the participants of the embassy were: Gamliel the Second, Joshua ben Hananjah (the disciple and colleque of Yohanan ben Zakkai), and Eleazar ben Azarjah (for a period *nasi* in stead of Gamliel the Second). The purpose of the embassy may be connected with the persecutions of the Jews under Domitian, and perhaps with the conversion to Judaism of a cousin of Domitian, Flavius Clemens. Akiba and Clemens might have got into touch. The result of the embassy is not obvious, Clemens was executed by the Emperor for Jewish superstitions. Perhaps the embassy met the senator Nerva, maybe the rabbis were still in Rome, when Nerva ascended to the throne. A result of the embassy might be the altered fiscus.

And then: Akiba and Simon bar Kochba. Akiba not only had confidence in Rome, he believed in God and in salvation from God. He saw part of the salvation in the zealous warrior Simon. He died as a martyr a few years after the fall of Bethar, Simon's fort. He was aware then of his mistake; Simon did not prove to be the king Messiah. By the way, it was not because of his messianic expectations that the Romans sentenced him to death. The reason was that he broke the Roman ban on studying Torah. Like Yohanan ben Zakkai, Akiba knew that Jewish necessity knows no Roman law. And the study of the Torah is a Jewish necessity.

Politics and theology. Or rather: politics because of theology. At least in two ways this holds true: 1) a minority has to be clever politicians, if they want to save their peculiarity. 2) Jewish theology implies a fundamental openness to the world. My last argument in this lecture is about the missionary urge in Judaism. This argument includes the universalism of the Old Testament and of Jewish tradition as such. It is an idea which could not be separated from that of the chosen people.

I shall only touch on the complex. In Leviticus ch. 19 different rules are handed down, among them rules concerning the poor and the stranger. In the concluding phrases the command goes:

> If a stranger sojourn with thee in your land, ye shall not vex him. But the stranger that dwelleth with you shall be unto you as one born among you, and thou shalt love him as thyself: for ye were strangers in the land of Egypt: I am the LORD your God (19, 33-34).

Love is universal, circumcision or no circumcision. But, of course, to the Rabbis to belong to the chosen people is a mercy and a happiness beyond measure. To offer the stranger to go inside the walls of Judaism is to love him.

The missionary urge in Judaism in the Second Temple period is a fact, though it is discussed if and to what extend Judaism proselytized systematically. Under the Maccabees, strangers were forced into Judaism, the example of the Idumeans being wellknown. The Pharisees and the scribes forced no one. I guess that the making of proselytes differed from place to place, from Palestine to Diaspora, from country to country, from town to town, and even from synagogue to synagogue.

Sometimes the gentiles themselves came to listen and ask questions, sometimes the Jews uttered the first word. The Sages held that the gentiles should come in the last days, when the glory of Jacob was restored, but some of them felt the necessity of active calling for mankind. The later Jewish maxime that by different ways man is led to God, but that there is but one way for the Jewish people, may have existed, too. The Sages were conscious both of the chosen people and of the whole world as God's creation.

Concluding Remarks

The catastrophy of 70 C.E., renewed during the fall of Bethar and the rise of Aelia Capitolina on the site of the Holy City was not only survived but surmounted by the Sages of Pharisaic stamp. The surmounting was not created over the night, the foundation had been laid and cultivated since Ezra, since the Babylonian exile, and even before; we would be right in pointing to Moses! They all worked for the life of the Jewish community. To protect this life strong walls were built. The men behind the Books of Moses, behind the prophets and the psalmists, all of them knew that the walls were not there to let life die. From the time of Alexander the Great with the excessive flow of Hellenism, the walls were of no less necessity than before. But from now on we meet men of wisdom who dare look out and take in new thoughts and forms, at the same time presenting their own tradition to strangers. Interaction takes place without the results of syncretism and assimilation; the walls are still there; but the windows, the doors, the gates become gateways through which you — Jew or gentile — can walk in and out without loosing your identity.

For all Jews to all time Jerusalem was the metropolis and the Holy City. A man like Simon the Just, as well as a Yohanan ben Zakkai or a Rabbi Akiba, not forgetting the almost heretic Rabbi Eleazar ben Hyrkanos, knew that there is a world not only outside Verona or Rome, but even outside Jerusalem. When Gamliel the Second tried to close some of the gateways to the world outside, he was for a time unwillingly released from his burdens as *nasi*. On the other hand, when Eleazar ben Hyrkanos was walking too much in the world outside, he was banned for a time from showing his curious countenance in the academy at Jabne. The gateways had to be in balance with the walls. For, as the Jew knows: 'On three things the world stands: on the Torah, on Worship, and on acts of lovingkindness.'

NOTES:

1. Josephus attributes the epithet 'the Just' to the first high priest named Simon. Likewise Megillat Ta'anit and Yoma 69a make Simon the Just a contemporary of Alexander the Great. Other sources indicate that Simon the Just was Simon II, who lived a century later. Cf. Loebs ed. of Jewish Antiquities VII, Appendix B.
2. Theophrastos, Hecataeos, Megasthenes and Clearchos. See M. Stern, 'The Jews in Greek and Latin Literature', in: *The Jewish People in the First Century*, Vol. II, p. 1101ff.
3. The origins of the anti-Jewish concepts, which dominate in Hellenistic-Roman times, are to be found in the Greco-Egyptian literature from the third century B.C.E. and onwards. M. Stern, *op.cit.*, esp. p. 1111ff.
4. The meaning is: you are not allowed to answer questions of Law while nude.
5. In Deut. 7, 16 and 12, 2.
6. The story about the statue in the synagogue of Nehardea is strange, but might be connected with other political circumstances. The statue in Nehardea was probably a picture of the Parthian king, 'Avodah Zarah 43b; Rosh Hashanah 24b.
7. The questions around the *fiscus judaicus* are discussed by P. Richardson and M.B. Shukster, 'Barnabas, Nerva and the Yavnean Rabbis', *JTS* 34 1983, p. 31-55. The problems of the fiscus are bound to the problems of the voyages of the Sages to Rome. See also G. Alon, *The Jews in their Land in the Talmudic Age*, Vol. I, p. 124-131.

BIBLIOGRAPHY:

Gedaliah Alon, *The Jews in their Land in the Talmudic Age*, Vol. I-II, Jerusalem 1980-1984.

M. Avi-Yonah, *The Jews under Roman and Byzantine Rule*, Jerusalem 1984.

Elias J. Bickerman, 'The Historical Foundations of Postbiblical Judaism', in: *The Jews. Their History, Culture, and Religion*, Ed. by Louis Finkelstein, New York 1949 a. 1955.

Judah Goldin, 'The Period of the Talmud', in: *op.cit.*

The Jewish People in the First Century, Vol. I-II, Ed. by S. Safrai and M. Stern, Van Gorcum 1974-76.

Emil Schürer, *The History of the Jewish People in the Age of Jesus Christ*, Vol. I-II, Revised ed. by Vermes, Millar and Black, Clark 1973-79.

Concerning the *fiscus judaicus*, important references are found in: Peter Richardson and Martin B. Shukster, 'Barnabas, Nerva and the Yavnean Rabbis', *JTS* 34 1983, p. 31-55. The authors discuss a comprehensive rabbinic material.